Oprah Winfrey Speaks

Insight

from the

World's Most

Influential

Voice

BY JANET LOWE

John Wiley & Sons, Inc.

New York • Chichester • Weinheim • Brisbane • Singapore • Toronto

This book is printed on acid-free paper. ∞

Copyright ©1998 by Janet Lowe. All rights reserved.

Published by John Wiley & Sons, Inc.
Published simultaneously in Canada

This publication is designed to provide accurate and authoritative information in regard to the subject matter covered. It is sold with the understanding that the publisher is not engaged in rendering professional services. If professional advice or other expert assistance is required, the services of a competent professional should be sought.

This book has not been prepared, approved, licensed or endorsed by Oprah Winfrey, Harpo Productions, or by any entity that creates, produces, or broadcasts *The Oprah Winfrey Show*.

Excerpts from *Working Woman* and *Ms. Magazine* are reprinted with the permission of MacDonald Communications Corporation. Copyright ©1998 by MacDonald Communications Corporation. For subscriptions call 1-800-234-9675.

Library of Congress Cataloging-in-Publication Data
Lowe, Janet
   Oprah Winfrey speaks: insight from the world's most influential
  voice / by Janet Lowe.
     p.   cm.
   Includes bibliographical references.
   ISBN 0-471-29864-6 (cloth : alk. paper)
   1. Winfrey, Oprah—Quotations. 2. Television personalities—
United States—Biography. 3. Motion picture actors and actresses—
United States—Biography. I. Lowe, Janet. II. Title.
PN1992.4.W56A3   1998
791.45'028'092—dc21
[b]   98-36572

Book design and composition by Anne Scatto / PIXEL PRESS

Printed in the United States of America

10 9 8 7 6 5 4 3 2

~ * ~

This book is dedicated to Tarah, Brandon, Alethea, J.D., and all the other young people who can take inspiration from Oprah Winfrey's life story.

~ * ~

Oprah Winfrey Speaks

Insight

from the

World's Most

Influential

Voice

~ ✳ ~

CONTENTS

PREFACE

There is an elite cadre of famous people who are recognized immediately, the world over, by their first names alone. Among them, however, there's only one that we all know intimately. Oprah is not just another famous entertainer. She's a friend to the world and a role model for all people, of any gender, of any race, of any group. Her warmth as a human being inspires and influences the millions worldwide who watch her daily yet never meet her in person. In 1998 talk show host Oprah Winfrey was voted the second most admired woman in America, with Hillary Rodham Clinton being the first. Oprah was followed by former First Lady Barbara Bush and former British Prime Minister Margaret Thatcher.[1]

The Oprah Winfrey Show entered its 13th season in 1998. By then the show had garnered 30 Daytime Emmy Awards and that year Oprah, at the relatively young age of 44, was honored at the Emmys with a Lifetime Achievement Award.[2]

"Oprah Winfrey arguably has more influence on

the culture than any university president, politician, or religious leader, except perhaps the Pope," wrote *Vanity Fair* magazine.[3] A *Newsweek* magazine columnist even posed the question: What if Brits could elect a monarch? Step up to the throne and accept your crown, Queen Oprah.

But Oprah's star status didn't just land in her lap. A daunting work ethic, excellent time management, amazing business acumen, and a massive dose of showmanship made her the number 1 television talk show host worldwide.

With 15 to 20 million viewers in the United States and exposure in 132 countries as far flung as Bangladesh, Cyprus, Mongolia, and Singapore, her afternoon talk show generates more than $260 million a year in advertising revenue. The take for Oprah's company, Harpo Entertainment, is about $120 million.

That, along with her other work, has made Oprah one of the wealthiest women in the United States. She is worth an estimated $600 million.[4]

In addition to the show, Oprah has a string of honors and achievements. She joins Mary Pickford and Lucille Ball as the only women to own their own movie production studios. She earned a Golden Globe and an Academy Award nomination for her performance in *The Color Purple*.

In 1996 Oprah was inducted into the Television Academy Hall of Fame during ceremonies in Orlando, Florida, along with actor Alan Alda, cartoonists William Hannah and Joseph Barbera, TV executive Barry Diller, pioneering TV news producer Fred Friendly, and the late sportscaster Howard Cosell.[5]

In 1993 she was named winner of the Horatio Alger Award given to people who overcome great adversity to become leaders in their field.[6]

Not only is Oprah successful, she is uniquely American. Black, southern, born out of wedlock and into poverty, she has faced many kinds of adversity.

Nevertheless, at a very early age she decided—she chose—to take charge of her destiny and become a woman of influence. Oprah got a job as a radio broadcaster while still a teenager, and postponed graduating from college to accept her first television news assignment.

Although Oprah's Chicago-based talk show was an immediate hit, she has had her share of career problems. Some of the show topics were of questionable taste and others were blatantly sleazy. She once interviewed a sexual surrogate who turned out to be a fraud who also had appeared on several other talk shows. After being castigated by the audience for being unfaithful to his wife, one young guest went home and committed suicide a few weeks later. And, of course, the famous beef with Texas cattle ranchers over a show on mad cow disease landed Oprah in court. (More about these issues later.)

Yet over the years Oprah's piercing honesty and heartfelt empathy won audiences and her stature grew. The most sought-after guests, from Hillary

Clinton to Michael Jackson, willingly appeared on her show. Although Princess Diana was never a guest, Oprah was invited to Kensington Palace to join the princess for lunch. It was a social rather than a business occasion.[7]

Furthermore, Oprah uses her show to make a safer and saner world. In 1990, the Year of the Child, for example, Oprah devoted many segments to issues such as children living in poverty, raising disabled children, and child sexual abuse. She testified before the U.S. Congress calling for a national database of all indicted and convicted child abusers. As a result, in 1993 President Clinton signed the National Child Protection Act allowing child care providers to conduct a national criminal background check on prospective employees.

Thanks to her daily television appearances, the world watches Oprah continually blossom and grow as the "diva of daytime discourse." Additionally, she is ever-present as an actress, a movie and television producer, philanthropist, and businesswoman.[8]

Oprah makes her personal philosophy well known—pro-choice on abortion; antiguns; tough on pornographers, drunken drivers, and smokers. She is equally tough on petty criminals, negligent mothers, welfare abusers, or anyone else who doesn't take responsibility for their own actions and lives.

Much also is known about Oprah's personal life, perhaps more than any other celebrity in our time.

Born in rural Mississippi, she spent her early years

with a strict grandmother and a terrifying grand-father. When she moved to Milwaukee to live with her house-cleaner mother, they were achingly poor. From age 9 she was sexually abused by several relatives and a family friend and at 14 she gave birth to a premature baby boy who did not survive. Later, to please a boyfriend, she experimented with cocaine. Oprah gained and lost hundreds of pounds of weight and for years she had difficulty finding and maintaining a healthy romantic relationship.

Many of these facts have been told publicly on her show, and although Oprah sometimes feared the repercussions from such sordid revelations, they only seemed to draw her audiences closer.

Has all this attention, power, and wealth over the years changed Oprah? Of course it has. We all change with time, and events change us. As might be expected, her private life has become more guarded as she becomes wealthier and more famous. Her shows have become slicker and more carefully orchestrated. Has the change in her been for the better? Oprah thinks so.

The lawyer who manages Oprah's business affairs, Jeffrey Jacobs, seems to agree: "She still has both feet on the ground. She just wears better shoes."[9]

This is the fourth in a series of books about the most successful contemporary Americans, portraits painted in their own words. The earlier subjects were Warren Buffett, the world's most successful investor; Jack Welch, chairman of General Electric and one of the world's most innovative managers; and Bill Gates, chairman of Microsoft Corp. and the world's greatest entrepreneur. Winfrey may at first seem out of place among these men, but in truth, she fits right in. She rose from humble roots to the absolute top of her profession. Like Buffett, Welch, and Gates, she restructured and redefined a job and even an industry in her own image. Like these three men, Winfrey is highly intelligent, blessed with lifelong good health and high energy, has faith in her own ideas, and is persistent in following her dreams.

The remarkable thing about Oprah Winfrey is how well she has been able to deal with success, fame, and wealth. As her story book life progresses, she continues to adapt, grow, and become a stronger, deeper, and more spiritual person.

∼

Before reading *Oprah Winfrey Speaks*, here are some guidelines on what to expect from the book. It will not be focused on the well-known details of Oprah's life and rise to stardom, although this information is presented to give the reader a better perspective on the comments. Rather, the book emphasizes the lessons that Winfrey has learned along the way—lessons many of us can profit from. Oprah has taught us a lot, and I've tried to capture as much of that wisdom as possible.

The book makes it clear that for all her popularity and good works, Oprah still struggles with everyday problems, family tragedies, programs that go wrong, bad-mood days, and personal shortcomings. She remains, after all, a human being, fallible like the rest of us.

But she does have more influence than the rest of us, and I've tried to explore Oprah's real role in our society, explain how she has been able to make an emotional connection and touch the lives of television and movie audiences everywhere.

Please remember that the quotations printed here were not uttered in the order in which they are listed. They have been grouped under topics and organized so that Oprah's philosophy and thoughts evolve, just as they would if you were having a conversation with her. To learn when and where Oprah made these remarks, please refer to the endnotes. To help readers understand the sequence of events, an extensive timeline is included at the end of the book.

This book was compiled and prepared without the authorization of Oprah Winfrey or the staff at the Harpo Entertainment Group. However a draft of the manuscript was sent to Winfrey so that she could review it, correct any factual errors, explain the context of the quotations, or make comments of her own on the events of her life.

Oprah Winfrey has been described in many ways: corny and manipulative; fearless and unpredictable; a copycat and an innovator. Not everyone agrees on her significance and value to society. But everyone does agree that Oprah is funny and always fun. And everyone agrees that she is the ultimate contemporary heroine—a disadvantaged women of color rising from southern poverty to become one of the wealthiest and most visible people in the world.

ACKNOWLEDGMENTS

Special thanks to Myles Thompson, Jennifer Pincott, Heather Florence, and Robin Goldstein at John Wiley & Sons, Inc., my literary agent Alice Fried Martell, my husband and helpmate Austin Lynas, and all the others who contributed to this book.

A WOMAN OF INFLUENCE

EVERYONE LISTENS TO OPRAH

It is said that the United States has become the most influential country in the history of the world because of this nation's ability to communicate our popular culture. When Athens, Rome, and Victorian England were at their zenith, there were no televisions, videocassettes, or World Wide Webs to spread their values to every village. Yet it is neither our elected representatives nor our technological geniuses who are doing the most communicating. President Bill Clinton may have political power; Microsoft founder Bill Gates may have economic influence; but Oprah Winfrey spends more time on television both listening and talking to both ordinary and extraordinary people, and that gives her a larger audience than either the world's top political leader or its dominant industrialists.

Writer Fran Lebowitz says "Oprah is probably the greatest media influence on the adult population. She is almost a religion."[1]

~

Oprah's community spills over borders:

"Every Euro-citizen can now watch Oprah Winfrey on his own national channel, dubbed or subtitled in his own language. There are no local equivalents, in spite of the limits that Europe imposed in 1991 on the import of American programs."[2]

~

Oprah Winfrey persuaded people to listen to her from an early age. She began reciting and performing at church and community events at age three. She could read and write before she entered kindergarten. After a brief but boring time in kindergarten, she sent her teacher a note: "Dear Miss New: I do not think I belong here." Miss New got the message and immediately advanced Oprah to first grade.[3]

~

Airline travelers once chose Oprah Winfrey as the person they'd most like to be seated with on a long flight. If they couldn't sit next to Oprah, they'd settle for Arnold Schwarzenegger, Ross Perot, Connie Chung, President Clinton, David Letterman, Dan Rather, Hillary Rodham Clinton, Madonna, or Boris Yeltsin.[4]

~

"When Ellen said 'Yep! I'm gay,' " wrote Mark Steyn in *The National Review*, "Oprah was by her side, guesting as (what else?) the star's therapist. She is, of course, therapist to an entire nation. If only it weren't so hard for the rest of us to get an appointment."[5]

~

Before she signed the contract to continue doing her show until the year 2000, Oprah thought long and hard. She had been in the talk show business for 21 years and was weary, but it was difficult to give up such a powerful platform. She chose to go on:

> *"I want to use television not only to entertain, but to help people lead better lives. I realize now, more than ever, that the show is the best way to accomplish these goals."[6]*

NEW WORDS IN THE LANGUAGE

In 1993 *Jet* magazine reported that the word "Oprah" had become part of the youth lexicon, meaning "to engage in persistent, intimate questioning with the intention of obtaining a confession; usually used by men of women, as in 'I wasn't going to tell her, but after a few drinks, she Oprah'd it out of me.'"[7]

~

Five short years after *Jet* spotted the new teen usage for Oprah's name, *The Wall Street Journal* and *National Review* magazine confirmed a new word among adults.

~

"This upending of tradition—from keeping one's heart under control to wearing it always loudly and tearfully on one's sleeve—has come to be known as Oprahfication, after the famous talk-show host who popularized public confession as a form of therapy," said a *Wall Street Journal* editorial writer.[8]

～

"Oprahfication doesn't refer to anything as piffling as a partisan creed or a stylistic voice; as denounced by *The Wall Street Journal*, it means 'public confession as a form of therapy,' but even that quote doesn't cover it: rather, Oprahfication has become the routine designation for nothing less than the wholesale makeover of the nation, and then the world," wrote *National Review*.

For example, Washington correspondents criticized a Clinton administration meeting in Ohio to drum up support for the bombing of Iraq as an "Oprah-style" town meeting.

"If only," the *National Review* countered. "Had Oprah, rather than Madeleine Albright, gone out to endorse bombing Iraq, Saddam would now be in the same enfeebled state as those Texas cattle barons."[9]

NOTE: For more on the Texas cattle barons, see "The Cow Row."

OPRAH'S ROOTS

ROOTS DEEP IN MISSISSIPPI

Oprah spent her first six years with her paternal grandparents, calling her grandmother "momma," and living in fear of her grandfather, Earless Lee.

> *"Always a dark presence. I remember him always throwing things at me or trying to shoo me away with his cane. I lived in absolute terror."[1]*

Oprah's grandparents kept pigs and chickens and grew much of their own produce on a plot so small it could hardly be called a farm. It was just a few acres, Oprah recalled. They had their own water well but no indoor plumbing. One of Oprah's childhood chores was to bring buckets of water to the house.

Oprah has been able to draw on her early life for much of her work, including a scene in the made-for-TV movie *Brewster Place* in which she had to feed a flock of chickens:

"I have more than sense memory, I have life experience of saying, 'here, chick, chick, chick.' I used to do it on my grandmother's farm when I was four years old. It's very therapeutic and boring. It's great in a movie scene for five minutes, but not so great if you have to do it every day."[2]

~

"Some of my fondest early memories are of my grandmother over a stove fixin' food for our daily feast. I grew up eating well. Cheese grits, homemade biscuits smothered in butter, home-cured ham, red-eyed gravy—and that was just breakfast. Smothered chicken, butter beans, fried corn, and corn bread was a typical weekday dinner. Sunday supper (when the preacher from the church down the road would often stop by) was a celebration. Food was the guest of honor, covering so much of the table there was hardly room for plates."[3]

~

Oprah's grandmother Hattie Mae Bullock, who is now deceased, was a strict but positive influence on the granddaughter she helped raise:

"I am what I am because of my grandmother. My strength. My sense of reasoning. Everything. All that was set by the time I was six."[4]

~

The often-told story that Oprah had no shoes until she was seven years old is untrue. Her grandmother provided her with two pairs of shoes each year, but because she lived on a farm and didn't dress up much, she wore shoes only when she went to the Faith-United Mississippi Baptist Church on Sundays.[5] Her grandmother tried to raise Oprah properly:

> "... some of my most comforting memories are of sitting between my grandmother's skirted knees while she scratched my head and oiled my scalp. It was our ritual, one we performed again and again, right there on the front porch—as did many a black girl growing up in the South. Today I know enough to know that comfort was about all that I was getting out of our little ritual, because it certainly wasn't doing my hair a bit of good. But it felt great at the time."[6]

~

Despite many happy memories of her early years, Oprah says her grandmother's discipline was unnecessarily harsh:

> "She could whip me for days and never get tired."[7]

~

> "I wanted to be a little white kid because they didn't get whippings. They got talked to."[8]

~

Oprah describes her parents' relationship as a "one-day fling under an oak tree."[9] They never married, and in fact Vernon Winfrey didn't even know Vernita, Oprah's mother, was pregnant until she sent him a copy of the birth announcement along with a request for baby clothes.

> "I was raised with an outhouse, no plumbing. Nobody had any clue that my life could be anything but working in some factory or a cotton field in Mississippi. Nobody—nobody. I feel so strongly that my life is to be used as an example to show people what can be done."[10]

~

> "There were certainly times as a child when I felt, 'My God, I wish I were like everyone else.' But as an adult, I celebrate my upbringing. I say, 'Thank goodness I was raised by my grandmother the first six years, then sent to live with my mother and then with my father. Because of the various environments I was exposed to, I am better able to understand what others have gone through."[11]

~

> "I don't think of myself as a poor deprived ghetto girl who made good. I think of myself as somebody who from an early age knew I was responsible for myself, and I had to make good."[12]

~

> "I was a little colored girl with 17 different barrettes in my hair, thinking I was Shirley Temple, getting up at church—'And little Miss Winfrey is here to do the recitation' and ladies saying, 'Hattie Mae, this

girl is gifted.' They were right and I believed them. I am where I am because of grace in my life. Being great depends on your willingness to get out of the way and let grace take over your life."[13]

~

The road that runs in front of the old farm in Kosciusko, Mississippi where she spent her first six years has been renamed Oprah Winfrey Road. The house itself is no longer standing.

GOING NORTH WITH MOTHER

When Oprah was writing her yet-unpublished autobiography, she discovered that though she has no memory of it, her mother had lived with her on the Mississippi farm until she was four years old.

Before Oprah started school, Vernita Lee became part of the great 1950s migration of poor black people from south to north. She moved to Milwaukee in search of work and a better life. Oprah stayed with her grandparents for several years more, until her mother sent for her. By then the bond between mother and daughter—delicate in any circumstance—apparently was damaged.

"I had my mother on our Mother's Day show last year [1987], and I could not hug her. Oprah Winfrey who hugs everyone could not hug her own mother. But we have never hugged, we have never said, 'I love you.' And yet we are both at peace with that. On

the other hand, I think that Maya Angelou was my mother in another life. I love her deeply. Something is there between us. So fallopian tubes and ovaries do not a mother make."[14]

〜

After moving to Milwaukee, Vernita had two more children. Oprah and her stepbrother and sister lived first in a boardinghouse then in an apartment. Her mother worked long hours cleaning houses, but never had much money. Oprah longed for a father and a traditional home life.

"I told the biggest lies about [my family] because I wanted to be like everybody else."[15]

〜

One of her elementary school teachers realized Oprah was gifted and felt he could help her by getting her a scholarship to a suburban school. When she rode the bus to an affluent neighborhood, along with all the maids who were going to clean houses, Oprah realized for the first time that she was poor. More than ever, she wanted her mother to be like June Cleaver, in the 1960s family situation comedy, *Leave It to Beaver*. But her mother was one of the maids.

"And she was tired. And she was just trying to survive. Her way of showing love to me was getting out and going to work every day, putting clothes on my back and having food on the table. At that time I didn't understand it."[16]

~

Oprah was devastated after her half sister, Patricia Lee, revealed to the tabloids that, at age 14, Oprah had given birth to a premature baby boy. Oprah had never spoken of the pregnancy publicly.

"The experience was the most emotional, confusing, and traumatic of my young life."

She had hoped to keep the matter private "until I was fully able to deal with my own deep emotions and feelings, so that I could share this experience" with other young girls trying to cope with sexual abuse.[17]

She didn't speak to Patricia for two years after that. Part of the stress between Oprah and her sister, who is seven years younger, was that they have far different recollections of their childhood. Patricia describes their mother as a very hardworking, dedicated mother and Oprah as a wildly out-of-control adolescent who was prone to exaggeration. Eventually Oprah invited Patricia, their mother, and several cousins to spend a weekend at the log cabin on her farm, so they could talk things out and heal old wounds:[18]

"I didn't feel I could continue to go on the air speaking to people about forgiveness if I couldn't do it myself. There was a lot of pain, a lot of stuff let out. But I did it so that we could go on and live with each other as women people."[19]

~

11

As for her relationship with her mother today:

"I forgive her for any anger and hostility, and she forgives me."[20]

~

Oprah bought her mother, Vernita, a new house in Milwaukee and insisted that she retire from her job as a hospital dietician, offering to double her salary for life.[21]

~

Oprah and her family continue to face tragedy. First, Oprah's longtime assistant Billy Rizzo, died of AIDS in 1988, then just a year later her half brother Jeffrey Lee died of the same disease.

Oprah had provided Jeffrey with some financial assistance before he was diagnosed with AIDS, but the two had a falling out over his lifestyle and his unwillingness to keep a job. Jeffrey gave a scathing interview saying that Oprah was unsympathetic to his plight and refused to help him. Although Oprah would not help her half brother directly, she did increase the money that she gave her mother so that she could support him if she wished to do so.[22]

Oprah also supplied money to help raise her sister's two daughters.

~

Despite the early difficulties, Oprah has a close family group that now includes her friends, her beau Stedman Graham, and his daughter, Wendy.

~

"My friends are my family."[23]

~

Her friends and family make holidays special. Oprah remembers the Christmas of 1990 with special pleasure:

> *"The farmhouse was finally finished and we decorated it with real evergreen garlands and holly boughs. The staircase was my favorite. It was woven with Christmas greenery from top to bottom. In fact, the whole setting was perfect—a snowy Christmas Eve with my family and many of the people I love most. Even the dogs were decked out in red bows."*[24]

FATHER

> *"I wanted a Daddy when I was in Milwaukee. I wanted a family like everybody else."*[25]

~

During fourth grade, Oprah lived with her father and stepmother in Nashville. Vernon Winfrey owned a barbershop and a grocery store, but he and his wife were childless and they welcomed Oprah into their home. When Oprah's mother planned to get married and expected to be able to provide a home, she asked her daughter to return to Milwaukee. But things did not go well, and by the time Oprah was 14 she was running away, stealing money from her mother and having sex with older boys. When Milwaukee juvenile authorities would not put Oprah in detention because their facility was overcrowded, her mother, in desperation, called Vernon Winfrey and asked him to come get his daughter.

Although her sister Patricia says Oprah cried and didn't want to go live with her father this time, Oprah now sees the move as her salvation:

> *"When my father took me, it changed the course of my life. He saved me . . . I was definitely headed for a career as a juvenile delinquent."*[26]

Vernon Winfrey agrees that Oprah was an unruly kid, but he set high standards for her because he knew she was capable. "She just wouldn't listen to her mother," said Winfrey. "She needed some discipline to make sure she got a good start."[27]

Like Oprah's grandmother Hattie Mae, Vernon believed children benefited from strict rules and hard work:

> *"My father's discipline channeled my need for love and attention into a new direction. He saved me. He knew what he wanted and expected, and he would take nothing less."*[28]

Oprah's father explained the household rules to her: "If I tell you a mosquito can pull a wagon, don't ask me no questions. Just hitch him up."[29]

~

Oprah's stepmother, Zelma, was "real tough, a very strong disciplinarian, and I owe a lot to her because it was like military school there. I had to do book reports at home as well as in school and so many vocabulary words a week."[30]

Her father—although she says she is not certain that he actually is her father—also explained the ways of the world to Oprah. He told her, "There are those who make things happen. There are those who watch things happen, and there are those that don't know what's happening."

Oprah decided to be one of those who make things happen.

~

She already was a seasoned speaker on the church circuit when she moved to Nashville, and public speaking continued to be a determining element in the development of Oprah's self-image and personality:

"I've been an orator really, basically, all of my life. Since I was three and a half, I've been coming up in the church speaking. I did all of James Weldon Johnson's sermons. He has a series of seven sermons, beginning with 'The Creation' and ending with 'Judgment.' I used to do them for churches all over the city of Nashville. I've spoken at every church in Nashville at some point in my life. You sort of get

*known for that. Other people were known for sing-
ing. I was known for talking."*[31]

~

It was just a few months after she arrived in Nashville
that Oprah, who had hidden the fact that she was
pregnant, gave birth to a son. He died within a week
or two and Oprah returned to school feeling that she
had a second chance on life.

Oprah has been resentful that her father didn't
seem to believe her and intervene when she told him
at age 13 that she was sexually abused by his brother
Trent. Vernon Winfrey said: "I know she feels that I
didn't handle it well. Trent was my closest brother.
We were torn."[32]

After Stedman Graham, Oprah's betrothed, flew to
Nashville to discuss the issue with his future father-in-
law, Vernon Winfrey visited his daughter at her farm
in Indiana. The two had a long talk, and he apologized
for not protecting her from abuse.

~

Oprah bought a new home for her father and is generous with both her parents. However, she says her
father doesn't ask for much:

*"The only thing he's ever asked me for was a ticket
to the Tyson-Spinks fight."*[33]

~

When she visits her father with her live-in fiancé,
Stedman and Oprah abide by Vernon's rules:

"We slept in separate bedrooms. I would absolutely not even try it. I wouldn't even dare try it! Are you kidding? We had bedrooms at opposite ends of the hall. 'Yup, Dad, I'm down here.'"[34]

~

When Oprah established scholarships in her father's name at Tennessee State University, she said:

"No person has had a greater influence in extolling the importance and value of a good education than my father. It is because of him that I am where I am today."[35]

~

However, Oprah's father fell under suspicion when a 28-year-old female college student accused him of exposing himself and demanding oral sex in exchange for financial help. The woman filed a $3 million civil suit against Winfrey, a former Nashville city councilman and church deacon. Oprah says she was appalled by the accusation:

"My father, Vernon Winfrey, is one of the most honorable men I know. In his professional and personal life, he has always tried to do what is right and help people. Since my childhood, he has set excellent standards that helped me succeed."[36]

A judge dismissed the charges against Vernon Winfrey for lack of evidence. Later, an attorney who represented the woman who made the accusation lost his license to practice and got 30 days in jail for soliciting $300,000 to drop the case. The lawyer allegedly told prosecutors, who were posing as representatives of Oprah Winfrey, that a large-enough payment "could take care of everything."[37]

YOU ARE RESPONSIBLE FOR YOUR LIFE

GET A GOOD EDUCATION

> *"If you grow up a bully and that works, that's what you do. If you're the class clown and that works, that's what you do. I was always the smartest kid in class and that worked for me—by third grade I had it figured out. So I was the one who would read the assignment early and turn the paper in ahead of time. That makes everyone else hate you, but that's what worked for me."[1]*

~

> *"The door to freedom is education. . . ."[2]*

~

> *"To those of us to whom much is given, we are compelled to do all that we can to save our young people. For to save ourselves, we must educate ourselves."[3]*

~

Oprah's teachers have been special to her.

"For every one of us that succeeds, it's because there's somebody there to show you the way out. The light doesn't necessarily have to be in your family; for me it was teachers and school."[4]

~

She aspired to become a fourth-grade teacher, largely because Oprah admired her own fourth-grade teacher, Mrs. Duncan.

"If I wasn't doing this, I'd be teaching fourth grade. I'd be the same person I always wanted to be, the greatest fourth-grade teacher and win the Teacher of the Year award. But I'll settle for 23 Emmies and the opportunity to speak to millions of people each day and, hopefully, teach some of them."[5]

~

One of her teachers in Milwaukee recognized her potential and placed her in "Upward Bound," a program that prepared talented low-income students for college. After that, Oprah rode the bus to Nicolet High School in Fox Point, a Milwaukee suburb. Although the experience revealed to Oprah how poor her family was, she still appreciated the attention of the teacher, Gene Abrams.[6]

~

To a group of young women in Chicago whom she has mentored, Oprah said:

"When we talk about goals and they say they want Cadillacs, I say, 'If you cannot talk [correctly], if

you cannot read or do math, if you become pregnant, if you drop out of school, you will never have a Cadillac, I guarantee it! And if you get Ds or Fs on your report card you're out of this group. Don't tell me you want to do great things with your life if all you carry to school is a radio."[7]

~

Oprah left Tennessee State University in her senior year to accept a full-time job on television, but later returned, completed a class project, and earned her degree in speech and drama. That year she delivered the commencement address.

BOOKS

"I learned to read at age three and soon discovered there was a whole world to conquer that went beyond our farm in Mississippi."[8]

~

"Books showed me there were possibilities in life, that there were actually people like me living in a world I could not only aspire to but attain. Reading gave me hope. For me, it was the open door."[9]

~

"Reading books is the single greatest pleasure I have. When we go on vacation, Stedman is the activity guy, and I'm always the girl with the book under the tree."[10]

Oprah held tight to her love of books despite the difficulties it caused her while she lived with her mother in Milwaukee:

> *"Not only was my mother not a reader, but I remember being in the back hallway when I was about nine—I'm going to try to say this without crying—and my mother threw the door open and grabbed a book out of my hand and said, 'You're nothing but a something-something bookworm. Get your butt outside! You think you're better than the other kids!' I was treated as though something was wrong with me because I wanted to read all the time."[11]*

> *"Getting my library card was like citizenship, it was like American citizenship."[12]*

Most people in the television industry thought it was a needless risk when Oprah Winfrey began her show's book club segments, and indeed, the show's ratings dipped at first. Soon they recovered, and in 1996 they doubled those of her nearest competitor, *Live with Regis and Kathie Lee*. When Toni Morrison was told that her 1977 Pulitzer Prize–winning novel *Song of Solomon* would be the second offering of the club, Morrison was puzzled: "I'd never head of such a thing, and when someone called, all excited, with the news, all I could think was, 'Who's going to buy a book because of Oprah?'

A million copies of that book sold, and sales of my other books in paperback jumped about 25 percent."[13]

~

The Oprah Book Club has become a powerful force in the publishing world. Being selected for the book club practically guarantees that 500,000 to 700,000 extra copies of a book will be sold.[14] The American Library Association credits Oprah for "single-handedly expanding the size of the reading public."[15]

~

Other books chosen by Oprah to discuss on the show have been *The Deep End of the Ocean*, by Jacquelyn Mitchard; *The Book of Ruth*, by Jane Hamilton; and Bill Cosby's books for children, *The Best Way to Play*, *The Meanest Thing to Say*, and *The Treasure Hunt*.[16]

> *"The best thing about it is the thousands of letters from people who hadn't picked up a book in 20 years. Some literally made me weep."[17]*

~

Oprah often recommends children's books. Some of those she likes are *Chicka Chicka Boom Boom*, by Bill Martin; *Richard Scarry's Best Word Book Ever*, by Richard Scarry; *Sesame Street: Another Monster at the End of This Book*, by Joe Stone; *Make Way for Ducklings*, by Robert McCloskey; and *The Girl Who Loved Wild Horses*, by Paul Goble.[18]

~

Oprah's production company has purchased film rights to several books chosen for the club, including Kay Gibbons's *A Virtuous Woman* and Toni Morrison's *Paradise*. Critics have described the arrangement as "very cozy," since a well-known book has a head start on publicity when it is made into a movie. Kate Forte, head of Oprah's movie production company, says there is no grand strategy here, "Except for the fact that everything we do is something that Oprah is really passionate about." Oprah also has purchased film rights to a number of books and scripts not featured in the book club.[19]

~

Not everyone appreciates Oprah's taste in books or her ability to cause sales to soar. She bounced basketball bad boy Dennis Rodman's booking from her show schedule because, in her opinion, his books, *Walk on the Wild Side* and *Bad as I Wanna Be*, crossed the line of acceptable taste.[20] After Oprah canceled Rodman's appearance, this item appeared on the Web site Bitch of the Week: "That Oprah Winfrey wields that sort of power—to take an unheard of book by an unheard of author, and [catapult] it into a million-seller, frightens the bejesus out of me. Who the hell is Oprah Winfrey? By contrast, if a respected book critic writes a rave review, one might expect a few thousand copies to sell. Oprah sneezes on the dust cover and entire forests quake in contemplation of the consequences."[21]

~

ROLE MODELS

Oprah Winfrey chose many role models as a girl. She admired historic black women such as Sojourner Truth, Harriet Tubman, Ida B. Wells, and Madame C.J. Walker. As a youngster she memorized and performed monologues of their writings or about their lives. When she reached her teens, she wanted to be just like Diana Ross and Tina Turner.[22] Perhaps because of her early heroines, Oprah emphasizes the importance of being a person of quality.

> *"The greatest contribution you can make to women's rights, to civil rights, is to be the absolute . . . best at what you do."*[23]

~

When she was given a Lifetime Achievement Award at the 1998 Daytime Emmys, television veteran newscaster Barbara Walters made the presentation. Walters said she personally takes credit for Oprah's success, since it was after seeing a Walters interview that Oprah told Miss Fire Prevention judges that she wanted to become a television journalist. When Winfrey tried out for her first television news job, she read like Walters would and sure enough, she got the job.

> *"We are all beacons of light for each other. I'm just glad that Barbara was there to be a beacon for me."*[24]

~

"The only thing greater than Oprah's accomplishments," replied Walters, "is the size of her heart."[25]

～

When she accepted her first Emmy Award in 1987, Oprah expressed her thanks to TV–pioneer Phil Donahue.

"Phil Donahue showed them that American women were interested in living their lives in the best possible way, and I thank Phil Donahue for that, for paving the way for me."

NOTE: For more, see "But Are You as Good as Donahue?"

～

Especially after she arrived in Chicago, Oprah strove to be a role model for young black women.

In 1986 she became involved in the Big Sisters program at the Cabrini Green project in Chicago. She invited the young girls to her home for pizza and slumber parties, took them on shopping sprees and a ski trip. The Big Sisters had one strict rule: Become pregnant and you're out of the program.

"We tell kids that if you want affection, you don't need a baby. Get a kitten instead."[26]

～

She realizes her success inspires others:

"It lets other women who look like me know that there are greater possibilities for them, too."[27]

What makes Oprah a worthy role model? Dr. Laura C. Schlessinger—radio's Dr. Laura—has one explanation: "She's determined to be the architect of her own life. And she doesn't use the past as the basis for her identity."[28]

LIBERATE YOURSELF

"I had to get rid of that slave mentality," Winfrey said when discussing the process by which she took charge of her business affairs.[29]

A slave mentality can sneak into all segments of life:

> *"I was raised subservient and not to think for myself. One day, my assistant said to me, 'You don't have on a slip.' Every morning of my life my stepmother would check me out to make sure I'd picked out the right socks, that everything matched. When I weighed 70 pounds, I had to wear a girdle and a slip every day. God forbid that somebody should see through your skirt! What are they gonna see? The outline of your leg, that's all! So I told my assistant, 'I don't wear slips any more and never will as long as I'm black.'"[30]*

> *"You don't have to have laws that say 'you can't come here or go sit there in this place in order to be a slave. The only thing that frees you is believing you can be free."[31]*

"It appears I have everything, but I have struggled with my own self-value for many, many years. And I am just now coming to terms with it," Oprah said at the time she put her autobiography on hold.[32]

~

"I'm finally ready to own my own power, to say 'This is who I am.' If you like it, you like it. And if you don't, you don't. So watch out, I'm gonna fly."[33]

~

Oprah takes pride in her heritage. In 1989, Oprah told a group of women:

> *"I come here tonight celebrating every African, every colored, black, Negro American everywhere, that ever cooked a meal, ever raised a child, ever worked in the fields, ever went to school, ever sang in a choir, ever loved a man or loved a woman, every cornrowed, every Afroed, every wig-wearing, pig-tailed, weave-wearing one of us."*[34]

~

> *"I wouldn't say I feel an obligation to speak 'for all blacks,' but I do feel myself as part of a tradition. I carry with me the voices of the women who have gone before me. When I speak for me, I also speak for them...."*[35]

~

Winfrey once scolded black people who turn against other blacks, or fail to maximize their potential, as falling victim to slave mentality. She encouraged these people to live in a way that honors their ancestors:

> *"I see self-hatred that makes us turn against each other and try to pull each other down. I see that and I think that Frederick Douglass [the great emancipator and communicator] does not deserve this. He did not teach the slaves to read by candlelight to see us at our banquets and meeting halls sit and try and tear each other apart. He does not deserve this!"*[36]

Yet because she did not relate well to the racially militant mood of the mid-1970s, her college years were not a happy time for Oprah.

> *"They [her college classmates] all hated me—no, they resented me. I refused to conform to the militant thinking of the time. I hated, hated, hated college. Now I bristle when somebody comes up and says they went to Tennessee State with me. Everybody was angry for four years. It was an all-black college, and it was in to be angry."*[37]

Oprah agrees with the Reverend Jesse Jackson:

> *"Excellence is the best deterrent to racism."*[38]

Oprah realizes that her success does not mark the end of racism.

"If other people perceive me to be representative of black people in this country, it is a false perception. The fact that I sit where I sit today, you can't deny there have been some major advances. But I'm still just one black woman."[39]

~

When Tiger Woods, the golfer with the fabulous smile who won the 1997 Master's Championship at the tender age of 21, was a guest on *The Oprah Winfrey Show*, he carried the dialog on race another step forward. Woods said it bothers him when people try to categorize him as an African American since his heritage is complex. "It does. Growing up, I came up with this name. I'm a 'Cablinasian.' "

Woods is one-fourth black, one-fourth Thai, one-fourth Chinese, one-eighth white, and one-eighth American Indian.[40]

~

Although she seldom has been called "nigger," like her character Sophie in the movie, *The Color Purple*, Oprah had an answer ready when it happened. On one of her first news stories for WTV in Nashville, she was sent to a segregated neighborhood to do a story. When introduced to a shopkeeper, Oprah reached out to shake his hand. "We don't shake hands with niggers down here," he said. "I'll bet the niggers are glad," she shot back.[41]

FINDING
HER NICHE

LET OPRAH BE OPRAH

When Oprah went to work at WJZ-TV in Baltimore, the station advertised her arrival on the television news scene with billboards, asking "What's an Oprah?"[1]

The campaign offended Oprah, but she must have asked herself a similar question:"Who is Oprah, and what will she become?" The answer to that question was influenced by a decision she made shortly after moving to Nashville to live with her father:

"I decided to be the best and the smartest."[2]

After that, it was just a matter of finding her own special niche.

~

Oprah's first job—during her high school years—was working in her father's grocery store. She didn't like the work and was glad when the opportunity to work as a radio broadcaster came along.[3]

Oprah's high school boyfriend Tony Otey says she

broke up with him because her school work, extracurricular activities, plus an on-air job at WVOL Radio were taking up so much of her life. There was no time for romance:

"One thing I remember most about Gail [Oprah used her middle name in high school] is that she knew what she wanted very early in life. She said she wanted to be a movie star. She wanted to be an actress. And I praise God that she's done that. She was willing to put aside a lot of other things. Back in the seventies, drugs had started entering the schools, and that kind of thing. We were involved in integration and those fights in those years. We were actively involved in that, but she knew what she wanted to do. She worked hard at it, and when her ship started to sail, she got aboard."[4]

～

At age 19, Oprah became the first woman and first African American to anchor the news at Nashville's WTVF-TV. After three years in that job, she advanced to a larger market, WJZ-TV in Baltimore to anchor the 6 o'clock news. After the show's producers decided her delivery of the news was too emotional, she was relegated to the morning show, *People Are Talking*.

"The minute the first show was over, I thought, 'Thank God, I've found what I was meant to do.' It's like breathing to me."[5]

～

"Sometimes you don't choose your career. It chooses you."[6]

~

People Are Talking was a success, trouncing Donahue in local markets. The show went into syndication and was picked up by about 12 cities, but it was not the hit nationwide that it was in Baltimore. Because Oprah was teamed up with a male cohost, she felt she wasn't fully able to be herself.

Seven years later she relocated to Chicago to host WLS-TV's *AM Chicago*. Within a month *AM Chicago* became the number 1 talk show in Chicago. Within five months Oprah's show was the third highest rated series in syndication, murdering the top-ranking Phil Donahue afternoon talk show. Before the year was ended the show was expanded to a full hour and renamed *The Oprah Winfrey Show*. Just five years after a career and personal crisis in Baltimore, 30-year-old Oprah was grossing $30 million and had millions of devoted fans.

When Oprah first became a talk show host, most talk shows were produced and aired locally. There were only a handful of nationally syndicated shows. By the 1994–1995 season there were 14 syndicated talk shows, and by the 1996–1997 season there were 24.

~

Although some critics see her as over-controlling, by having the final say, Oprah ensures that her show reflects her personality:

"Nothing gets booked if I don't want it. We [she and the staff members] are a team; but if I don't want to do it, it doesn't make sense to book it, because a lot depends on my interest and energy."[7]

⁓

". . . my head hurts when I have to be in any situation where people are being phony. So if I can't be myself and take my shoes off when my feet hurt, then I'm not going to do very well."[8]

⁓

Not only is the talk show Oprah's natural niche, it's ABC's as well. The 4 P.M. show is considered essential by many television stations, since those who watch Oprah stay on the same channel for the 5 P.M. news.

In addition to finding her right place in television, Oprah has configured herself as an important brand name. Marketing expert John Grace, director of New York–based Interbrand, says of Oprah, "She's a very important brand in our culture. Her presence as a brand is embodied by trust, human-to-human connections and realness. Her audience has come to believe Oprah is real and she is telling the truth."[9]

⁓

At a time when Oprah was striving to restructure her show so that it would be more inspirational, she faced stiff competition from Jerry Springer. Springer became the number 1 show in February 1998, partly due to staged fistfights between guests. After protests from community groups, Springer agreed to stop coaching guests to get physical when discussing problems.[10]

Oprah regained her leading position later, but throughout the year she and Springer contended for the top slot.

NOTE: For more on the talk show wars, see "Why Oprah Seldom Watches Television."

~

Oprah's style leads her to say whatever her gut tells her to say. For example, she once told a teenage runaway to "quit your whining." From Oprah, who had plenty of teen problems of her own, the comment carried authority.[11]

~

"The rest of the talk shows are just tissue. Oprah is Kleenex," said one television analyst.[12]

~

The secret to Oprah's success was clear to Chris Clark, her boss on her first television job on WJB-TV in Nashville. If you want people to love her, "You had to let Oprah be Oprah."[13]

BUT ARE YOU AS GOOD AS DONAHUE?

Oprah Winfrey's first ratings victory over Phil Donahue, the master of the talk show world, was sweet.

"I like Phil Donahue, but I have to admit it feels good to beat him. For the longest time, I couldn't go

about doing my job without people saying, 'Yeah,
you're good. But are you as good as Donahue?'"[14]

⌇

One newspaper reporter thought he knew why Oprah
was so popular. "For some reason she comes over more
sincere than Donahue. I know you won't believe this.
Phil majored in sincerity in college. He set the standards for sincerity by which everybody is judged.
Oprah out-sinceres Phil."[15]

⌇

Deborah Tannen, a Georgetown University communications professor, says that Donahue's show was mostly
"report talk," which is typical of the way most men
hold conversations. In report talk, the focus is on information. Tannen says that Oprah naturally adopted
"rapport talk," the give-and-take style that character-
izes women's conversation. In this kind of discussion,
the emphasis is on self-revealing intimacies.

"When my book *You Just Don't Understand: Women
and Men in Conversation* was published," Tannen
said, "I was lucky enough to appear on both Donahue and Oprah—and to glimpse the differences
between them. Winfrey related my book to her own
life; she began by saying she had read the book and
'saw myself over and over' in it. She then told one of
my examples, adding, 'I've done that a thousand
times'—and illustrated it by describing herself and
Stedman."[16]

36

~

Oprah believes that passion makes the difference:

"I'm a person who lives my life with great passion, and I think that comes across on the camera."[17]

~

One media critic claims that Donahue and Winfrey are neither sincere nor passionate. "In Donahue, the veteran, and Winfrey, the newly arrived, we have two masters of the con. In bowing their audience's string, they make full use of the fact that they are not white women. Both are skilled actors, each knows when to caress a wrist or touch a shoulder or milk an emotion just so."[18]

GIRLFRIEND TO THE WORLD

"People out there think that I'm their girlfriend; they treat me like that. It's really amaaazing.*"*[19]

~

"She's like the one friend you trust, the one you know has good taste," said Maryann Koehl, a fan waiting in line to see *The Oprah Winfrey Show*. "You stick with a girlfriend like that, you know."[20]

~

Girlfriends defend one another, as Oprah did for Sarah Ferguson, the former wife of British Prince Andrew, after she was a guest on the show:

"It was like talking to me. I would have been kicked out of the palace too."[21]

~

Oprah, who's never been much of a cook and admits that she is too disorganized to be a tidy housekeeper, still has a lot in common with most women of today.[22] She's had a career since she was a teenager. Her main focus is not on cooking and cleaning but rather on better relationships with friends and family, self-actualization, and finding solutions to the myriad problems that press in on modern women and their families.

Nevertheless, it is Oprah's way of relating to others that forges the friendship bond. In a sociology research paper published on the Internet, Jennifer Hollett explained that TV talk show hosts such as Oprah Winfrey create a "para-social relationship" in which a crowd of strangers have the illusion of a face-to-face, intimate relationship with the star of the show.

"This 'intimacy at a distance' is such that people count television characters, especially TV personas such as talk show hosts, amongst their own friends and family members," writes Hollett. "The informal, ritualized, and interactive style of talk show hosts encourage this through a variety of ways. A conversational style of speech, a direct gaze at the camera, or direct reference to the audience gives the viewers an apparent role in the interaction. This allows them to feel that they have a one-to-one relationship with her. It is this phenomenon that motivates TV viewers to mail Winfrey 5,000 letters each week, and inspires fans to make comments like the following, 'Oprah is me. We're both black, we're both the same age, we treat people the same way. That could be me.'"[23]

It's not surprising that Oprah chose "I'm Every Woman," by Whitney Houston, as her show's theme song.[24]

~

One of Oprah's dearest friends is poet Maya Angelou. Oprah gave Angelou a 65th birthday party, a two-day event to which 400 guests were invited.[25] For Angelou's 70th birthday, Oprah booked a party boat for a seven-day Caribbean cruise. Among the 150 guests who set sail from Fort Lauderdale, Florida, were composer Quincy Jones, Coretta Scott King, Andrew Young, and Hall of Famer Ernie Banks. Before the cruise, Oprah requested a list of her guests' dress, shoe and other apparel sizes, favorite brands of makeup, and other information. Each night a gift arrived—matching pajamas for couples, hats, and picnic baskets. When the boat docked for a party on a private island in Key West, singer Patti LaBelle performed from an elevated, rotating birdcage, in honor of Angelou's book, *I Know Why the Caged Bird Sings*.[26]

For many years Angelou didn't celebrate her birthday because it falls on the same day Martin Luther King was assassinated.[27]

~

To Angelou, Oprah is more than a friend. If she had a daughter, Angelou says, "Oprah, beautiful, tough and bodacious, is the kind of daughter I would want to have."[28]

Angelou tells what makes Oprah special to her:

"The little girl's laughter that erupts unexpectedly mid-sentence should not lure any observer into believing her to be childish, nor should the direct glance encourage any to feel that she is a hardened sophisticate. She is an honest, hardworking woman who has developed an unusual amount of caring and courage."[29]

~

Oprah and fast-rising talk show host Rosie O'Donnell helped put to rest the rumors that they were feuding and that competing women can never be friends.

"Oprah and me having a feud?" Rosie asked incredulously. "How ridiculous. I love her and respect her. As far as I'm concerned, Oprah rules."[30]

Rosie has distinguished herself from other talk shows by focusing on wholesome fun, entertainment, and information. If Oprah is the Queen of Confession, Rosie is the Queen of Clean. Rosie won the ratings race in Los Angeles, the nation's second biggest TV market, in 1997, the first time Oprah had not led the L.A. ratings since the show debuted in 1986.[31]

Still, Oprah had kind words for O'Donnell:

"Rosie is great at being Rosie, and I'm Oprah, and I'm great at being Oprah. And we're both very good on television."[32]

When Rosie won an Emmy for Best Talk Show in 1998, at first she seemed a little confused and crestfallen. Although she didn't say as much, she looked as if she felt guilty for having snatched the prize from *The Oprah Winfrey Show*, which had gathered nine Emmys in that category, including the previous four years in a row. Oprah and Rosie tied for the title of Best Talk Show Host.

> *"We both feel that this is God's work. We thank you for allowing us to have this calling."*[33]

∼

At times, supporting other women has caused rumors to fly about Oprah. After she appeared on the *Ellen* "coming-out" show as a psychiatrist, gossips suggested that Oprah herself was a lesbian:

> *"I appeared on Ellen's show because I wanted to support her in her desire to free herself. I am not in the closet. I am not coming out of the closet. I am not gay."*[34]

∼

Later DeGeneres appeared as a guest on Oprah's show, where many audience members voiced their opposition to Ellen's coming out.

> *"A lot of people said me being on your show . . . was me promoting lesbianism. I simply wanted to support you in being what you believe was the truth for yourself."*[35]

∼

Even so, if you're a girlfriend to the world some surprising things happen. When *Ladies' Home Journal* ran an Oprah look-alike contest, part of the prize was a trip to Chicago to appear on *The Oprah Winfrey Show*.

The winner, selected from 4,000 contestants, was very excited. "I'm gonna look at her and say, 'Girlfriend, I'm so tired of people telling me I look like you,'" said Jequin Stitt, 32, a clerk at the Flint, Michigan, water department.[36]

Only problem is that Jequin Stitt was not a woman but rather a female impersonator. In fact, said Stitt, he was undergoing a sex change.

"I'm not lying to the public," he claimed on a local television interview. "You know, because I am going through some changes."[37]

The magazine did not withdraw the prize. "We don't believe in sexual discrimination," explained editor-in-chief Myrna Blyth.[38]

~ ✳ ~

THE LEADING F.O.O. (FRIEND OF OPRAH)[39]

Gayle King, the Hartford, Connecticut, television personality, is Oprah's closest personal friend.

"She was there when I got married and she was there when I got divorced and she was there when my children were born," says King. "We're very, very close. And I'm absolutely nuts about her."[40]

~

Oprah once explained how their friendship began:

"I was an anchorwoman, and Gayle was a production assistant. One night [in 1976], there was a terrible snowstorm, so I invited Gayle, who was then living about 35 miles away, to stay at my house. She did—and we sat up and talked until dawn! Ever since then, we talk every day, sometimes three or four times."[41]

"But I don't have underwear," Gayle protested when Oprah invited her to stay over.

"I do, and it's clean," Oprah replied.[42]

~

Oprah explains why she and Gayle have remained friends for more than 20 years:

"In spite of all the things that have happened to me, we laugh every night about one thing or another. She absolutely keeps me grounded."[43]

~

When people first meet King, they sometimes are surprised by how much she talks and acts like Oprah. The friends even look somewhat alike.

"They assume that the way I talk and act, I'm copying her," King says. "They don't realize that we've known each other since we were 21 and 22, and we got to be like this together. I tell Oprah, she's taken my best stuff."[44]

~

King was born in Chevy Chase, Maryland, and lived the sort of life that Oprah yearned for as a child in Milwaukee. Gayle's father was an electronics engineer and her mother a homemaker.[45] She graduated from the University of Maryland with a degree in psychology.

King started her career as a production assistant in Washington, D.C. and Baltimore, where she went on the air. She moved first to Kansas City, Missouri and then on to Hartford, Connecticut in 1981. For a brief time before it was canceled, she cohosted an NBC daytime talk show with Maury Povich called *Cover to Cover*. When King was offered her own syndicated talk show, she says that Oprah encouraged the move and in fact at one time offered her the opportunity to join Harpo Productions in Chicago. King turned Oprah's offer down because she wanted to stay in Hartford where her children could see their father regularly:

"... [Oprah] was very supportive and remains supportive. And it's in my contract that I never compete against her in the afternoon, for two reasons: One—I don't want my butt kicked. . . . I'd like to have some semblance of dignity, and Two—I didn't want to add to that best-friend-competing-with-best-friend tabloid crappola."[46]

~

The Gayle King Show often follows *The Martha Stewart Show*. Stewart's program focuses on projects for the house and home, while King's half-hour focuses on the people in the home.

"I'm convinced you can do a show about normal people," says King. "There aren't any new topics. Every damn thing has been done, so our challenge is presenting it in a way that people will not mind seeing it again."[47]

~

"I think one of my biggest assets is that from the time I was a little kid, I asked a lot of questions," says King. "They used to call it being nosy. I prefer to call it inquisitive. It's not psychology, it's natural curiosity. I'm fascinated with what people do, why they do it, and how they do it."[48]

~

Oprah and Gayle have a similar approach to life:

"I don't like doing things halfway," says Gayle. "I don't like being mediocre."[49]

~

Like Oprah, Gayle speaks her mind. When her show first made its debut, her colorful way of expressing herself got King in hot water with mobile home dwellers and people with dental problems:

"We will have responsible people talking about responsible things in responsible ways [on the show]. We're looking for people with all of their teeth. Not people from trailer parks. I'm looking for articulate people. I will not do things that embarrass or humiliate people or embarrass or humiliate me."[50]

A reader of the *Atlanta Journal and Constitution* responded with a letter to the editor:

"I have a few questions for King before I tune in. Is that 'people with all their teeth,' or 'people with a $5,000 bridge to cover the spaces'? If I live in a trailer but not in a park, does that count? If I am toothless and live in a trailer park, does that make me twice as 'irresponsible' and 'inarticulate'?

"I have a suggestion for King. Better call Oprah for some advice, pronto," he wrote.[51]

~

King is the divorced mother of two children. Her daughter, Kirby, 12, and her son, William, 11, call Oprah Auntie O. There were rumors that their close relationship and the generous gifts Oprah gave the family contributed to Gayle's divorce from Yale-educated lawyer Bill Bumpus after 13 years of marriage.

But an Internet-fueled rumor went even further, implying that Winfrey and King are lovers.

"Yeah, they say that Oprah broke up my marriage and that I'm why Oprah and Stedman aren't married." King laughed and shook her head at that. "Anybody who knows how much I love men would really find that funny. Besides, although I'm not gay, I don't have any problem with the lesbian lifestyle, and neither does Oprah, so if it were true, we'd just say so."

Besides, King added, "You know how Oprah is; she goes on that show and talks about everything. Don't you think she'd talk about that?"[52]

~

Stedman Graham has no worries about Gayle and Oprah. When he appeared on Gayle King's talk show, he told her, "I think it's therapeutic for Oprah to have someone she can talk to and tell everything about her day and everything about her week, and you know, you are that person; you are that special person [that she never has the] feeling she has to hold something back."[53]

~

Does King ever feel she is in Oprah's shadow?

"People always amaze me by asking, aren't you jealous of Oprah? And I say, why would I be? I'm happy with my own life, and I'm so thrilled for her. When I visit Oprah I'm wined and dined and chauffeured around in a limo. And when I come home and can't remember where I parked the car at the airport or trip over the kids' toys, I think the visit was great, but I really like my life too."[54]

~

"I never feel I'm in her shadow," says King. "I feel like I'm in her light. . . ."[55]

~ ✳ ~

OPRAH'S BEST SHOWS

Some of Oprah's shows have become classics in the television world. She once did a program on women who bore children by their own fathers; during it she called an offending father for an interview from his prison cell, then ended up calling him slime. But she also confronts many difficult issues face to face.

In the first year her show was nationally syndicated, she picked up her crew and moved production to Forsyth County, Georgia, for what may be her bravest show ever. Oprah asked a group of local citizens why, for more than 75 years, they had not allowed a black person to live in the county.

One bearded man said that if blacks moved back to Forsyth County, it would become a rat-infested slum like his former Atlanta community, because "blacks don't care."

"You mean the entire black race?" asked Oprah.

"You have blacks and you have niggers," the man replied. "The blacks stayed at home during the march. . . . The niggers are the ones who marched. And if the niggers come in here, it's going to be nothing but a slum area."

Some white residents of Forsyth County in the audience booed at the man's comments.

During the show, black civil rights leaders picketed outside the restaurant where the show was taped. Several protesters were taken to jail. After the show, Oprah was asked how she would feel about spending the night in Forsyth County. "Not very comfortable," she replied. "I'm leaving."[56]

~

Later, when she did shows on the Ku Klux Klan, she said she didn't expect to reform their thinking.

"I don't try to change people. I try to expose them for what they are."[57]

~

On a cheerier note, the guests on her show have included First Lady Hillary Clinton; Michael Jackson (the first interview he'd granted in 14 years); Janet Jackson; Duchess of York Sarah Ferguson; golfer Tiger Woods and his father, Earl; former Beatle Paul McCartney; Ellen DeGeneres; Chicago Bulls basketball star Michael Jordan, and the venerable Barbara Walters, whom she made bawl. Pop singer Celine Dion and her entire family sang on Oprah's show.[58]

~

About some of her favorite interviews:

John F. Kennedy Jr.: "I remember sitting in my chair and talking to myself, just keep breathing."

The Artist Formerly Known as Prince: "Now I call him his highness."

Barbra Streisand: "I didn't want it to be just one of those kvelling interviews . . . I wanted to give her her propers first, then we could go on."[59]

~

Hanson, a pop music trio from Tulsa, Oklahoma, who are adored by millions of preteen girls, appeared on the show when Oprah was taping temporarily from Amarillo, Texas. A group of girls from Bivins Elementary School were invited to be in the audience, and 9-year-old Savannah J. Peeples wrote an account of the experience for the Amarillo *Globe-News*, where her mother is a reporter:

"Oprah said we were the biggest crowd since the Beatles. She talked a little bit about Hanson and introduced them. Hanson is a group of three brothers from Tulsa, Oklahoma. They are: Isaac, who is 17; Taylor, who is 14; and Zac, who is ll. Zac looked me right in the eye. I'm not kidding. It was so entirely cool."[60]

Savannah also got to be close to Oprah: "I got to talk to Oprah, but they probably edited it out. Then Oprah hugged most everyone in the front rows including me. It was a good hug. I said, 'You go, Oprah,' and she said, 'You do, too.' It was fascinating."[61]

~

While interviewing diminutive actor Dudley Moore, Oprah noted that he usually dated women who were much taller than he:

"Aren't there some technical problems posed by your habit of always wanting to sleep with taller women?"

After pausing, Moore replied, "Well, most of their length seems to be in their legs. Luckily."[62]

~

Oprah asked Boy George about his practice of dressing in women's clothing:

"What does your *mother* think when you go out?"

"She says she never thought she'd be proud to have a son dressed up like a transvestite," he replied with a frown.[63]

~

"I think many times you can ask the wrong questions. I asked Sally Field if Burt Reynolds wore a toupee. She didn't like that. I saw her face just kind of glaze over."[64]

Hurriedly, Oprah asked another question and the show went on.

~

One of Oprah's most notorious shows focused on the question of whether the size of a man's penis is important to his sex partner. Oprah sure seemed to think it does:

"If you had your choice, you'd have a big one if you could! Right? Bring a big one home to Mama."[65]

OPRAH AND ME—TWO GUESTS TELL OF THEIR EXPERIENCES

Appearing on *The Oprah Winfrey Show* is exciting for most guests. But not all shows turn out the way guests hope they will, especially since an appearance on Oprah can create incredible expectations. Misunderstandings occur, and even Oprah can have a bad day.

Richard Lederer, a San Diego–based linguist, learned the hard way to not pin his hopes on Oprah. This is Lederer's account of what happened:

Brrriiinnnggg. "Good morning, Mr. Lederer. My name is Jane Johnson (not her real name), and I'm a producer with *The Oprah Winfrey Show*. We've been seeing your bloopers all over the Internet and we'd like to do a show about them. Wednesdays is when we do our tapings at Harpo Studios here in Chicago, and we're looking at November 6 for your appearance."

"Well, sure," I agree, as I peel myself off the ceiling while still managing to clutch the telephone. "I'll be happy to be interviewed by Oprah. But you've apparently been reading bloopers from my two earlier *Anguished English* books. Are you aware that a third book of fluffs and flubs, *Fractured English*, is just about to be published?"

"No, Mr. Lederer. We didn't know that, but we'll be happy to feature your current book on the show."

My heart leaps when I behold a life-altering, career-changing chance like this. A producer calls on behalf of the woman who has the hottest finger on the hottest button in the book publishing industry. And she phones at the very moment—October 1996—when the presses are about to give the world the only kind of book I write that can actually be a national best seller. It's simply the grandest opportunity to publicize my books that I can ever have—worth more than all the other serendipitous chances that have ever entered my life.

Jane explains that for the lead-in, Chicago schoolchildren will act out a few of the language bloopers I've found. I then will have seven to ten minutes on the air with Oprah, talking about some of the funnier bloopers in my books.

By all the gods of writing. Seven to ten minutes with Oprah Winfrey. "O frabjous day! Callooh! Callay!" I chortle in my joy. I call my editors, who promise to print 100,000 additional copies after the segment is aired.

So, I fly out to Chicago. A fellow named Rudolph, pale from his sunless existence, meets and greets me at O'Hare and walks me to a stretch limo. I am whisked to the Omni Hotel, were I stay, sup and breakfast, courtesy of *The Oprah Winfrey Show*. In the morning, another stretch limo takes me to Harpo Studios for the taping.

Jane greets me and escorts me to the green room to wait to be on the show. Hardly have I arrived when she, ashen faced, tells me, "Mr. Lederer. We're terribly sorry, but we won't be able to use the lead-in tape. I thought the tape was so cute, but the senior producers say that the segment makes it look as though the children themselves have perpetrated the bloopers, and they're concerned about parental reaction.

"But don't worry," Jane says with a pasted-on smile. "This is just a taping, so we'll reshoot the lead-in for the actual airing and be just fine."

Woe is I, I think. Now we've lost the chance for the lead-in tape to energize Oprah and the studio audience. Not good, not good.

When trouble comes, it comes not singly but in legions. Next Johnson informs me that Oprah's stepmother, the central woman in her childhood, died that morning. Of all the days I could have been on the show of shows, I have to appear on the very day the unfortunate woman slips her mortal coil. For perfectly understandable reasons, Oprah is tired and flat that morning. And—the horror!—the first two segments go overtime!

"Don't worry," says the producer with the pasted-on smile. "Your segment is not thematically tied to the others. We'll put your interview on another show, just as long as Oprah is wearing a red dress that day."

Finally, the time arrives. Oprah strides on to the stage and speaks to her staff.

"What! We've got *another* segment? I gotta get outta here to the funeral."

I understand her having to rush off to her stepmother's funeral, but what does "What, we've got another segment?" mean? Does she know anything about my books? Is she prepared?

"Okay," Oprah says. "So we're doing a feature with Richard Lederer."

She pronounces my name Leed-er-er rather than Led-er-er.

Hoo boy. Oprah Winfrey, Queen of Talk Show Queens, doesn't know how to say my name! Perhaps she hasn't been briefed! Could that loud sucking sound I hear be my career going down the you-know-what? Oprah, I grieve for your loss, but you make more than $50 million a year. You're here on the set, so please, please give me five minutes, and you will change my life and you will get my books of language fun into the hands of a gazillion readers.

Mind you, I would have gladly changed my name to Leederer at this point, but in the name of truth, I correct her. "Excuse me, Oprah, It's Lederer."

Suddenly, some of the blooper headlines flash on to the screen.

Fried chicken cooked in microwave wins trip. Flaming toilet seat causes evacuation at school.

Oprah and I banter a bit about them. I wait for her first question: "So, Richard, what is your favorite headline blooper?"

But no question comes. All is silence.

I fill in the dying air. "Yes, Oprah, I love capturing two-headed headlines, and my favorite is the one that led off a golfing story: Grandmother of eight makes hole in one."

A burst of laughter from the audience. Some energy flows back into the studio. I await the next question. But Oprah doesn't have any questions, and all the air a solemn stillness holds.

"Well, Oprah, I collect all kinds of goofs and gaffes," I chirp. "A parent once wrote this excuse note to school: 'My son is under doctor's care and should not take P.E. today. Please execute him.' And my most famous student blooper may be 'Sir Francis Drake circumcised the world with a hundred-foot clipper.'"

More chuckles, followed again by an echoing wall of silence. Oprah closes the casket lid on the interview after just two-and-a-half minutes.

"Fabulous, Mr. Lederer!" jubilates the producer with the pasted-on smile. "You did great. We'll call you within two weeks, by November 20, to let you know when in December we'll air your interview."

The November deadline arrives. No word from the show. The rest of November crawls by, and then December (punctuated by a signed form letter: Thank you for being on *The Oprah Winfrey Show*) and then January. No news is bad news.

I call my publicist and ask her to check with the producer to see if and when the segment will air.

"Richard, Richard. I can't do that," she explains. "We're talking about *The Oprah Winfrey Show* here. We're talking the biggest. We wouldn't want to jeopardize any future opportunities for our other authors. You do understand, don't you?"

Of course I do. It's been nearly two years since that fateful day in Chicago, and I have never heard from the producer. My two-and-a-half minutes of fame are sealed tight somewhere in videotape limbo.

So how do I feel about the experience? Sad that my work will not receive an endorsement from the face that launched a thousand scripts. Would I do it again? Absolutely. Oprah, if you happen to be taking time off from reading all those books piled on your night table and happen to read this, I forgive your staff for throwing me overboard in an emergency. All you have to do is call and I'll fly back to Chicago, without benefit of airplane. You're a great woman, Oprah. But please remember that the name is Lederer.

NOTE: Richard Lederer's most recent books are *Crazy English* (Pocket Books) and *The Word Circus* (Merriam-Webster).

~

On the other hand, Debra Dickerson, who was a guest on an Oprah segment called "Make Peace with Your Hair," had a great time.

"From the moment she and I took our seats, we talked nonstop, when we were on the air and off. She held my hand and, repeatedly, stroked my unprocessed hair (I am black, like my hair) to see what it felt like. With cameras on, she squeezed my hands in different ways to signal when I was babbling, when to take a breath, when to shut up so she could talk. Surrounded by her audience, I felt as if I had stumbled upon a raucous gathering in a ladies' room where women who have just met become instant confidantes."[66]

MESSAGE OF THE MOVIES

Oprah dreamed of being an actress since she was a child. Then the producer of the daytime television soap opera, *All My Children*, was a guest on Oprah's show in Baltimore. Oprah expressed her love for the soap with her usual enthusiasm, so the producer got her an "under-fiver" (under five minutes) appearance on the show. It was her first professional acting role.[67]

Quincy Jones, who coproduced *The Color Purple*, discovered Oprah on a visit to Chicago where he watched television while having breakfast in his hotel room. Making the movie was the happiest time of her life. Oprah then knew she was an actress.

"I got the bug!," Oprah squealed after she was nominated for an Oscar for her role as Sophia.[68]

When she signed a deal with the American Broadcasting Company (ABC) in 1995 to produce six made-for-television movies under the banner "Oprah Winfrey Presents," she gained enormous control over her acting career.[69] Oprah has tried to make movies that deliver a meaningful message to all her audiences. Many of her dramas focus on life in the black community.

> *"There's a whole reality outside of what most people know, where the black community functions on its own, where people own businesses, where people care about their property and their children and pay their taxes. The point of having your own [production] company is that you can show that."*[70]

After the television movie *The Wedding*, about an interracial marriage, aired on ABC in the winter of 1998, Oprah's America Online Web site, Oprah Online, was flooded with messages from black and white persons who wanted to discuss racial issues.[71]

Oprah played the role of LaJoe Rivers in the made-for-TV movie, *There Are No Children Here*, although ABC originally wanted Diana Ross for the role:

> *"Diana said she didn't want to do it because it didn't offer enough hope. I felt the book was reality. There's always hope. I didn't grow up in the projects, but I am*

the perfect example of someone who came up from zip,
I mean zippola, Mrs. Outhouse herself here."[72]

In her made-for-TV movie *Before Women Had Wings*,
Oprah revisited the subject of child abuse and how
children can rise above it:

> *"It shows us that no matter how victimized you may*
> *feel in your own life, if there is someone who is willing*
> *to show that they love you, it can give you wings."*[73]

~

> *"I love a movie that makes you feel so deeply that*
> *you want to open your heart just a little bit wider."*[74]

OPRAH'S ACTING CREDENTIALS

TELEVISION MOVIES
> *The Women of Brewster Place*, 1989
> *Pee-Wee Herman's Playhouse: Christmas Special*,
> 1988
> *Listen Up: The Lives of Quincy Jones*, 1990
> *There Are No Children Here*, 1993
> *Before Women Had Wings*, 1997

FILMS
> *The Color Purple*, 1985
> *Native Son*, 1986
> *Throw Momma from the Train*, 1987 (A special
> performance of Oprah playing herself.)
> *Beloved*, in production, to be released October
> 1998

> *Guide to Black Excellence*, produced by *Ebony/Jet* magazines, 1991
>
> *Oprah: Make the Connection*, 1997

NOTE: Oprah also owns the movie rights to *Kaffir Boy*, Mark Mathabane's autobiography of growing up black in the ghettos of South Africa.[75]

Oprah may have wished she hadn't appeared on Pee-Wee Herman's show after the children's show comedian was arrested in 1988 for exposing himself in an x-rated movie theater. But she was only 1 of 13 guest stars, a list that included Frankie Avalon, Annette Funicello, Magic Johnson, Cher, and Whoopi Goldberg. And to borrow a phrase from Rosie O'Donnell, who knew?

OPRAH THE
CHIEF EXECUTIVE
OFFICER

HARPO

"Focus on this," said an insider at Harpo Entertainment Group. "She owns the show; she owns the production company; she owns the studio; and now she owns a major part of the distributor."[1]

~

It may be appropriate that Oprah named the company after herself, spelling her name backwards. Oprah represents the emotional, theatrical side of her personality. Harpo shows that Oprah has a flip side—that of a savvy business executive. Her greatest business talent has been identifying, hiring, and holding on to people who could create the media empire that Oprah wants. Harpo runs *The Oprah Winfrey Show*, plus prime-time specials, made-for television movies, and children's specials, all for ABC television. The majority of the employees at Harpo are women, and many are black.

~

In the summer of 1984, Oprah's longtime agent had negotiated a four-year contract with ABC with terms that were good, but they weren't making headlines. Later, Oprah said, three different ABC executives stopped her in the hallway to tell her what a great guy her agent was. She was puzzled that they thought he was so marvelous. If he were truly representing her interests, she asked herself, would he be so popular? She fired her agent and replaced him with Chicago entertainment lawyer Jeffrey Jacobs.

"I'd heard Jeff is a piranha. I like that. Piranha is good."[2]

~

Jacobs began working with Oprah shortly after she moved to Chicago, and gradually spent more and more time on her business. Finally in 1987 he closed his practice and joined Oprah full time. In 1988 Oprah took over the management of her show from Cap Cities/ABC and Jacobs was put in charge of running Harpo.

"He's the visionary. I just have the sense to know when his vision is doable for me."[3]

~

Under Jacobs's tutelage, Oprah has reinvested a substantial portion of her earnings in Harpo, building a 100,000-square-foot, $20-million production facility that takes up an entire block on Washington Boulevard near Chicago's West Side restaurant and grocery supply district. Although she has a relatively small staff of about 135 people, almost all of the business functions of the organization are performed in-house. By operating her own company, Oprah's income increased, but she also has greater freedom to set her own schedule and develop her own projects.

"He took the ceiling off my brain."[4]

~

Jacobs says that Harpo is truly an unusual company. "We are not structured like a typical Hollywood company." "Oprah is very hands-on."[5]

~

Furthermore, Oprah is the chairman and chief executive officer. She has no outside investors or board of directors to whom she must report:

"We have created a truly independent, vertically integrated production company. We own our facility; we do our own development. We have the wherewithal, both financially and creatively, to go into any area we want. It will be as big as we want it to be, depending on what we want to do."[6]

~

But according to Oprah:

". . . we want to stay small, like Steven Spielberg's Amblin [Entertainment]. I can't deal with a big bureaucracy."[7]

In 1997 the Harpo Entertainment Group had sales of $150 million, a 7.1 percent increase over the previous year. *The Oprah Winfrey Show* accounts for about 40 percent of the revenues of its syndicator, King World Productions.[8]

Thanks to her extraordinary ratings and the world-wide reach of her show, Oprah has enormous leverage when negotiating contracts.

Forbes magazine reporter Robert La Franco says, "Oprah has been ingenious about the way she's structured her operation. Basically she's said, 'Don't just pay me a salary, but let me participate in the profits as well.'"[9] The occasional suggestion that she may quit the show helps her get the deal she wants.

King World, Oprah's syndicator, is an aggressive, some even say cutthroat company, which also handles *The Geraldo Rivera Show*, *Wheel of Fortune*, *Jeopardy*, the popular TV news magazine *Inside Edition*, and a 1998 show to be hosted by comedian Roseanne.[10]

The 1994–1995 season illustrated how profitable a talk show can be. King World grossed $20 million a week in revenues on the Oprah show. The show cost only $200,000 a week to produce, so there were plenty of profits to share.[11]

Roger and Michael King run King World, which was founded by their father when television was in its infancy. Jim Coopersmith, president of WCVG-TV in Boston has worked extensively with the King brothers and describes them as street smart:

"I like street people. They have a reverse chic style," explains Coopersmith. "They are not Grant Tinker [former head of NBC], with the $2,000 suit, the 32-inch waist, and the Gucci loafers. They are big, healthy guys who look more like wrestlers. They're not like studio guys who come in with their Armani shorts and have nicer tushes than their wives. I hope I never get into a barroom fight, but if I do, I hope it's with the King brothers on my side."[12]

~

When Oprah negotiated the contract for 1999–2000, she was granted options to purchase 500,000 shares of King World stock at an exercise price of $39.31. Winfrey already had options to buy 1.55 million shares. The new deal would make Winfrey the largest holder of King World shares, owning as much as 5 percent of the company.[13]

~

In addition to Harpo Enterprises, Oprah owns a significant stake in Granite Broadcasting, a small New York–based media company that owns 11 television stations and 1 radio station. With such geographically diverse properties as KEYE-TV in Austin, Texas; KSEE-

TV in Fresno, California, and WTVH in Syracuse, New York, Granite reaches 8 percent of all television-watching American households.[14]

Granite was the 1995 *Black Enterprise* Company of the Year and is number 7 on *Black Enterprise* magazine's Industrial/Service 100 List.[15]

> *"I don't invest in anything that I don't understand— it makes more sense to buy TV stations than oil wells."*[16]

∼

Oprah's leadership style has been called "confident and personable."[17] People who work for her describe Oprah as a perfectionist but fair.

> *"To me, one of the most important things about being a good manager is to rule with a heart. You have to know the business, but you also have to know what's at the heart of the business, and that's the people. People matter."*[18]

∼

Oprah works hard and is very dedicated, as is her staff. Although Harpo Entertainment has the usual share of management problems, Oprah seems to inspire loyalty:

"People adore her," explained Dan Santow, a former producer on the show. "They give up their lives to her. People who work there get divorced, put off having kids, have no outside lives. Because everything, all your time and energy, is given to Oprah."[19]

~

"I would take a bullet for her," Mary Kay Clinton, a producer on the show, once claimed.[20]

~

Unlike so many other entertainment personalities, however, Oprah keeps a firm grip on the tiller, even to the point that she has been called a "control freak." She may have learned from comedian Bill Cosby that she should sign all checks. Before he and his wife Camille took control of his finances, Cosby unknowingly gave away about $3 million.[21]

"It's all about fear," Oprah has admitted.[22]

~ ✳ ~

TROUBLE IN OPRAH CITY

"I never took a business course. I run this company based on instinct. I'm an instinct player, an instinct actor—and I use it to guide me in the business. I think one of the things that makes me a good employer is that I was an employee for such a long time. I know what it's like to be called to the general manager's office. So what I try to do more than anything is just be fair. That really is the basis of my management style."[23]

~

In 1994, not long after Oprah made dramatic alterations in her exercise and eating habits, turmoil broke out at her Chicago studio. After three key staff members resigned (not all of them voluntarily), Oprah apparently wished she'd had more management training:

> *"I used to always say, 'I never went to business school,*
> *and I've never read a business book.' But now I think,*
> *maybe I should have read a few."*[24]

~

Employees complained that producer Debra DiMaio, whom Oprah had known since her days in Baltimore, was treating other staff members badly.[25]

The accusations put Oprah in a painful position, since DiMaio was largely responsible for recruiting Oprah from Baltimore to work in Chicago and could take credit for much of the show's success. Winfrey liked DiMaio and trusted her.

Oprah once gave DiMaio a six-carat diamond bracelet with a card reading "brilliance deserves brilliance.[26]

Yet the tension on the show grew and complaints got louder.

"Everyone probably thought we were so happy to be working at Harpo, we all sat around singing 'Kum Ba Yah' all day," said a former producer. "No way."[27]

A group of employees demanded a private meeting with Oprah and aired their feelings. After a fiery, closed-door session with Oprah, DiMaio resigned. DiMaio is reported to have received a $3-million plus settlement when she left.[28]

"Debbie was cruel," said one staffer who insisted on remaining anonymous. "She would dress down someone in front of everyone else. The bottom line is, Oprah had to know it. And she allowed it. In Oprah-speak, Oprah was an enabler to Debbie and the problems. It was a good-cop, bad-cop kind of thing. The staff is much happier now."[29]

~

But DiMaio's departure wasn't the end of the trouble. Soon after DiMaio left, Oprah's personal assistant and her publicist resigned as well. Publicist Colleen Raleigh, who had been with the show eight years, sued Oprah, saying that she did not receive the $200,000 in severance, $17,250 in unpaid salary, and about $6,000 in vacation pay she had been promised on quitting.[30]

Eventually the case was settled out of court for an undisclosed sum.[31]

Although many staff members welcomed the changes, DiMaio would be missed. "Whatever else she may be," said former Harpo producer Dan Santow, "[DiMaio] has the best instincts for good stories in the industry."[32]

~ ✳ ~

OPRAH'S WORK SCHEDULE

For years Oprah maintained an amazing, daunting work schedule.

"My schedule is very hectic, but it's exactly the kind of life I've always wanted. I've always said I wanted to be so busy that I wouldn't have time to breathe."[33]

~

A reporter asked Oprah if she was a workaholic:

"Yes, ma'am, I am. This is all I do. I do this and I do it till I drop. I work on weekends. I go as many places as I can to speak. I get home, and I say, 'What am I supposed to do here?'"[34]

~

Perhaps so that they can keep pace with their boss, the staff of *The Oprah Winfrey Show* is reported to consume more than 200 pots of coffee daily.[35]

~

After a grueling schedule of taping shows, public speaking, and charity events, in 1988 Oprah realized she was exhausted and should be more judicious about the way she spent her time.

> *"I used to take every phone call from a guy who said he would jump off a building if I didn't talk to him. But I no longer feel compelled to aid every crazy. For two years I have done everything everyone asked me to do. I am now officially exhausted."[36]*

~

After several vacations with Stedman Graham in which she was unable to relax, Oprah realized she worked exceptionally hard to make herself feel worthy of love. Change wasn't going to be easy for her.[37]

> *"I'm trying to create more balance, spend more time with my boyfriend and concentrate on the things that are important. Because all the money in the world doesn't mean a thing if you don't have time to enjoy it."[38]*

~

Although Oprah's schedule is lighter, she still works diligently. Monday through Wednesday, Oprah arrives at her studio at 6 A.M., where she exercises in the gym, and afterward has her hair and makeup done for a 9 A.M. taping. She then goes on camera for an hour-long show, holds a postproduction meeting, then tapes a second show at 11 A.M. After lunch, Oprah conducts production and business meetings in her office. She works for part of Thursday in her Chicago office, signing hundreds of checks each week and finishing paperwork. The remainder of the week is spent at her Indiana farm, where she relaxes, reads scripts, and does less structured work.

With all of her projects, Oprah produces approximately 220 hours of new television programming each year.[39]

"I go into the closet in my makeup room and I just close the door. Here, standing among the shoes, I'll just close my eyes and pause for a minute to re-center myself. Because after I tape two shows, I know that there will be six people outside my office wanting to see me about one thing or another."[40]

~

To save time and energy, Oprah now uses an autopen to sign letters and autographs. While the autopen is an enormous convenience for her, the signature is virtually of no monetary value to autograph collectors.

~

Oprah has a stunning view of Lake Michigan from her Chicago apartment, but until she moderated her work schedule, she wasn't able to appreciate it:

"Before it was just a view. And from season to season I would never see daylight. I'd come in to work at 5:30 in the morning when it was dark, and leave at 7:00 or 8:00 when it was dark. I went from garage to garage. This morning, I actually took time to enjoy the sun rising over the lake while I was drinking my cup of coffee. I actually allowed myself to see the sun reflected off the water and make it look like glass." [41]

Oprah finds her Indiana farm an especially restful retreat. There, she walks in the woods, does Tai Chi Ch'uan by the pond, grows her own collard greens, and curls up by the fireplace to read a book:

"I've realized it's very simple things that make me happy, but that I have to be open to happiness. I have to want to be happy rather than just busy. And once I am more willing to be happy, it becomes easier for me to feel the happiness." [42]

"I believe you can have it all. You just can't have it all at one time." [43]

ON LIVING WITH FAME AND FORTUNE

WHAT IT FEELS LIKE TO BE FAMOUS

"People have this fear of success. They're afraid if they get it, they can't keep it. I don't have a fear of it at all. Everything you do in life indicates how your life goes. I don't want to go all spiritual on you, but I just have always had this sense of connection. I was always a very eloquent child, and when I was 12 years old, I was paid $500 to speak at a church. I was visiting my dad and I remember coming home that night and telling him that was what I wanted to do for a living—to be paid to talk. I told my daddy then and there that I planned to be very famous."[1]

~

In 1986, when Oprah's show shot up in the ratings and she was nominated for an Oscar for her performance in *The Color Purple*, she was ecstatic:

"I mean it's tre-tre-double-mendous! It's my time to have fun, fun, FUN."[2]

Then the consequences of fame set in:

"There are moments, like in a bathroom stall at O'Hare Airport, you hear, 'Is that her?' 'Did she gain the weight back?' 'She's shorter than I thought.' Once I walked out and three women applauded. That is when I knew: I am famous."[3]

"People think they know you, that they're your friends, which is great. But you're also never allowed to be private. You never, ever, ever, have moments to yourself, and you're always conscious that people are looking at you."[4]

"I've developed a great respect for fish, I'll tell ya, because I've lived my life in a fish bowl."[5]

Fame can have its destructive side, as it did when a Toronto, Canada, tabloid newspaper ran an erroneous story claiming that Oprah's fiancé, Stedman Graham, had a homosexual relationship with a cousin. The cousin denied ever talking to *News Extra*. Stedman and Oprah filed a $300-million, six-count federal defamation lawsuit against the publisher, who also was being sued by Rod Stewart and Sylvester Stallone for stories the entertainers said were both false and incredibly offensive. Oprah and Stedman won their case by default when the newspaper shut its doors and its attorney did not show up in court.[6]

~

Graham admits that Oprah's eminence was hard for him, until he learned to deal with it. "I went through some rocky times in learning to cope with all of the attention and occasional trash journalism," he said, "but I realize now that Oprah's rise to fame was probably the best thing that could have happened for both of us. It forced me into examining myself and the influences on my life and to confront my private fears and insecurities. As Maya Angelou has written: 'Pressure can change you into something quite precious, quite wonderful, quite beautiful and extremely hard.'"[7]

~

Oprah agrees that the "celebrity trip" can be difficult:

"I understand why so many others have fallen apart, or turned to sex, drugs or alcohol. If you believe what you read about yourself, it will destroy you. I used to write back to critics, telling them I'm not a sleaze. Now I don't. I've learned how not to be controlled by the frenzy."[8]

~

Friends have helped Oprah come to terms with the problem. Bill Cosby told her there would come a time when the negative media attention would not bother her any more:

"And when that happens, he told me, you'll know that you've grown up. He was right, too. Because if

I've discovered anything during this whole process, it's that the only difference between being famous and not being famous is that people know who you are. Inside, I haven't changed a bit."[9]

~

Except for one thing. Fame has made Oprah less trusting of people.

"If you bring flowers to my house, you gotta sign an agreement that says you're not gonna come in there with a camera. That's after my whole house ended up in the National Enquirer."[10]

~

"I was hoping that this would not have happened to me. I was talking to Barbra Streisand about this and she was saying, 'Don't you have confidentiality agreements?' And I go, 'Well, then, doesn't that make people feel like you don't trust them?' And she said, 'But you don't.' So I now have moved to that ground I never thought that I would."[11]

~

On the bright side, famous people get invited to fabulous places. When President and Mrs. Clinton entertained the Japanese emperor and empress, Oprah was on the guest list. Also invited were Barbra Streisand, Peter Jennings, Ted Turner, Jane Fonda, and clothing designer Diane von Furstenberg. When she met the emperor and empress, Winfrey was speechless: "I didn't know what to say. And it was one of the few times."[12]

Oprah gave her view of fame to 1998 graduates of Wesleyan University:

"For me, greatness isn't determined by fame. I don't know if you want to be famous. I don't know if you want to go to the bathroom and have people say, 'Is that you in there?' 'What is she doing?' That is the price of fame—and then reading about it in the tabloids. I don't know if you want that for yourselves, but I do believe that what you want is a sense of greatness. What Dr. King says, greatness is determined by service."[13]

~

How does she find privacy? Oprah and Stedman once went to Wyoming and helped a friend herd cattle. The next day she was so sore she could hardly walk.

"But I don't believe the Enquirer *was anywhere around. It was very private."[14]*

SUDDENLY RICH? NO GUILT

When a Nashville radio station sponsored the Miss Fire Prevention beauty contest, 17-year-old Oprah Winfrey entered. The judges asked her what she would do if suddenly given $1 million. No altruistic answer here:

"I'd be a spending fool!"[15]

She won the crown.

~

At more than $600 million, Oprah's personal worth exceeds the gross domestic product of a small country. Which one? There are several, but they are small and rather obscure. They include the nations of Belize, Cape Verde, Comoros, Djibouti, Grenada, the Marshall Islands, Palau, and Saint Lucia.

~

"I have never felt a moment of guilt about what I have."[16]

~

"The external part of my life—where I live and what I drive, and what kind of panty hose I wear and can afford, and that kind of stuff—none of that stuff in the end means anything. The thing I'm most proud of is that I have acquired a lot of things, but not one of those things defines me. You know. I look at magazines or tabloids. And it's just—it feels like something outside of myself. It doesn't feel like me. It doesn't feel like who I am."[17]

~

"I'd like to set the record straight and let people know I really am not defined by dollars. I would do what I'm doing even if I weren't getting paid. And I was doing this when I was getting paid much, much less. At my first job in broadcasting, my salary was $100 a week. But I was just as excited about making that amount of money and doing what I love to do as I am now."[18]

~

"Experience, and not just a little heartache, has taught me money buys convenience and conveniences. I'm not knocking it either, but life's true meaning is about the time you can spend comfortably with your mate—and with yourself."[19]

~

She may not be defined by money, but Oprah publicly thanked her fans for making her a very rich woman. She had no qualm about wearing a fabulous diamond necklace and earrings to Oscar night.

"A lot of people offered to lend me jewelry for the night, but I didn't need it, honey—I got my own."[20]

~

Being rich doesn't save a person from an occasional embarrassment. Oprah says her most humiliating moment was at the 1986 Academy Awards, when she was nominated for an award for her supporting role in *The Color Purple*:

"The Academy Awards are like the biggest prom night of your life, so I spent hours before getting done, done, done—hair done, nails done, toes done. Anything that could get done, I got done."[21]

Oprah had hired a "chi-chi-poo-poo"[22] dress designer to make her a gown, and at the last fitting the designer decided the skirt needed to be tighter around the knees. The next day as she was dressing for the awards,

Oprah could not get the gown on. The seamstress had taken the skirt in from top to bottom. In desperation she lay on the floor while her friends pulled the dress up over her hips. She could get up and down only with help, or sit in her chair at the awards ceremony by continually pulling down on the collar of the dress. Finally Oprah got settled in her seat.

> *"Just then I heard the voice of God. 'You are not going to win this award!' he said, 'because you cannot get up to accept it!' So I knew before anyone that Angelica Houston was going to win the Oscar that year. You've heard the expression killer dress. Tell me about it."*[23]

~

For those who think Oprah's fame and wealth is just a matter of luck, she says:

> *"Luck is a matter of preparation meeting opportunity."*[24]

A SPENDING FOOL

As she predicted, Oprah became a spending fool when she struck it rich in Chicago.

Apparently she enjoys nice cars. Among the various luxury automobiles Oprah has owned is a Mercedes 560 SEL and a light-blue Jaguar Cabriolet—a convertible. She sometimes drives a pickup truck at her farm. Stedman gave her a classic 1958 Mercedes for her 40th birthday, but she later sold it, after giving up on learning to drive a car with stick shift. Oprah also buys cars for others—at least two employees and Stedman's grandmother.

While vacationing in Miami, Winfrey says she got "all dolled up, then jumped in her new Aston Martin convertible." She turned heads as she drove to the gasoline station:

"It was fun. I felt like a chickey babe."[25]

$\sim$

For times when a car isn't adequate, Oprah has a private jet. She also bought $200,000 worth of thoroughbred horses for her Indiana farm but couldn't ride them because they were too high spirited.

$\sim$

Earlier in her life Oprah poked fun at things that were "chi-chi-poo-poo," but she got over that. Now Oprah enjoys her wealth and has a wardrobe, jewelry collection, and several homes that could definitely be described as "chi-chi-poo-poo."

While working in Chicago, Winfrey stays in her sophisticated 57th-floor apartment on Chicago's Miracle Mile.

She bought the apartment from Evangeline Gouletas Carey, a Chicago real estate mogul who later married former New York governor Hugh Carey. Oprah paid $850,000 for the apartment, which takes up an entire floor of a skyscraper. It has a wine cellar, a sauna, and a crystal chandelier in the closet. The apartment overlooks Chicago's popular Oak Street Beach. It has a media room with a giant-screen projection TV and stereo system and silk draperies on a motorized system that opens or closes them at the touch of a button. She has a telescope, but "of course, I never look into other people's windows."[26]

Chicago interior designer Laurie Cowall worked with Oprah on putting together the white-on-white decor. The apartment is adorned with the work of black artists such as that of painter Arlene Case.[27]

~

When giving instructions on how to reach Oprah's 160-acre farm near Rolling Prairie, Indiana, a minimart clerk explained, "Drive all the way through [the village of] Saugony Lake, and it will be the first castle on the left." A little country humor there—it was the *only* castle.

Oprah says she loves the Indiana retreat because she spent her early years on a farm. While the countryside has the feeling of the rural South, especially in the spring and summer, The Farm, as she calls it, is nothing like her grandmother's shanty. A two-hour drive from Chicago, The Farm makes a flashy statement among the other modest farmhouses. Oprah's place cost $750,000, and then she invested another $250,000 in improvements. Pine trees line the driveway that leads up to a turreted, gray-stone, French-style chateau. On the grounds there is a helicopter pad, a swimming pool, tennis courts, and a riding stable.

Except for race car drivers who hang out around Indianapolis, not many celebrities share Oprah's love for Indiana. The exception is rocker John Mellencamp, but his home in Bloomington is far, far south of Oprah's estate. Just the same, *Mother Earth News* lists Indiana as one of the ten best places to live the good life in America. "This is real Middle America: church-going, square-dancing, hog-raising country where folks don't lock the farmhouse door or feel they need to count their change at the feed store."[28]

∼

Others may not lock up, but Oprah probably does. Fans often come looking for her farm, ruining her privacy. A large sign on the fence proclaims that this is "The Farm." And: "If you weren't invited, don't come in here."

Sturdy rail fences and a dozen or so surveillance cameras fend off unwelcome visitors. One way to get a look at Oprah's farm is to buy the video, *Oprah Winfrey: Make the Connection*. It was filmed partially on The Farm, with many bucolic outdoor scenes. Some of the video was taped in the Harpo studio in Chicago, and the rest is set along the Lake Michigan waterfront near Oprah's highrise apartment.

∼

On occasion, Oprah may find the neighborhood around her farm too countrified. In 1996 she wrote to LaPorte County officials complaining about the beat up condition of the roads. "I've witnessed the continuing deterioration of the roads surrounding and en route to my home," she told them. "I have never seen roads anywhere in such disrepair."

After the letter was read at a commissioner's meeting, one official joked that the multimillionaire used a helicopter, not local roads, to travel between her Chicago residence and The Farm. Another commissioner suggested that Oprah's letter be auctioned off to raise money for the road repairs. Many residents of Rolling Prairie, population 114, were offended by the commissioner's comments and sent a letter to the local newspaper apologizing. "We sincerely hope that Ms. Winfrey does not take the rude comments of two public officials as the norm for LaPorte County."[29]

The letter apparently was effective. At this writing, the road to The Farm seemed to be in good repair.

$\sim$

Winfrey also has an 85-acre mountain retreat in Telluride, Colorado, a remote Old West gold-mining town perched 8,745 feet high in the Rocky Mountains. Her majestic log-and-stone chalet, which also has a turret, is surrounded by some of the most stunning scenery in America. She paid $1.4 million for the house in Telluride's Mountain Village, then bought an adjacent 80 acres of pine and aspen forest for an extra sum.

Oprah met her trainer, Bob Greene, at The Peaks at Telluride, a luxurious hotel and spa frequented by the likes of Christie Brinkley and Whitney Houston. The

Peaks is renowned for its delectable low-fat food, such as a handcrafted pizza with basic pesto, Portobello mushrooms, caramelized onions, and eggplant for 267 calories and 2 grams of fat. The spa regime includes such exotic pleasures as eucalyptus herbal steam rooms and a morning ritual, "Wake Up to Oneness." Those who rise early enough to attend the class greet the day with Native American–inspired chants and dances.

～

Oprah is legendary for her gift-giving, both at Christmas and whenever the mood hits her. Not only was she maid of honor at producer Mary Kay Clinton's wedding, she paid for both the wedding and the honeymoon.

～

Christmas/Hanukkah/Kwanzaa at *The Oprah Winfrey Show* can get outrageously expensive. Producers, one year, decided to draw names for gifts, but for the sake of moderation agreed to limit the price of a gift to $250. That year the Christmas party was a black-tie dance at the Four Seasons Hotel, with dancing lessons given the week before.

At an afternoon-long luncheon the day after the party, staff members competed to present Oprah with the most original and imaginative gift. Oprah received an antique tea set, antique trunk, antique bible, antique violin, antique traveling kit, and a set of false eyelashes actually worn by Lucille Ball when she taped *The Lucy Show*. One producer presented Oprah with a numbered print depicting the life of the first black person to achieve sainthood, St. Martin de Porres.[30]

A producer who attended the party described the gifts Oprah gave to her staff.

". . . Oprah handed Beverly [her personal assistant] a small box. Inside was a brochure for a Jeep Cherokee. Beverly looked perplexed, but before she could even ask for an explanation we heard honking from outside the window. Then we heard Oprah's theme music blaring from the street, 'I'm Every Woman.' We ran to the window and there before us, with its lights and radio on, was a shimmering black Jeep Grand Cherokee. It was for Beverly. Another one of Oprah's aides was leaning against it, smiling slyly."[31]

Other producers received diamond earrings and luggage with a $10,000 travel gift certificate inside; senior producer Debra DiMaio received a year's certificate for once-a-month dinners with friends in Montreal, Paris, London, and other cities, all expenses paid. Unfortunately, DiMaio, Beverly, and a lavishly gifted publicist were gone from the staff six months later.[32]

~

Despite her wealth, Oprah maintains a practical streak. She can buy designer stockings every day of the week if she wants to, ". . . but sometimes Walgreen's wear better."[33]

CHARITY

"With all this fame and money, I have to do something more than buy shoes."[34]

~

"I'm generous to the people I know and to some people I don't know, if I feel their cause or their purpose has true meaning, and that they will benefit *from the money."*[35]

~

One Christmas Oprah heard from her friend Maya Angelou, who is a member, that the famous Glide Memorial Church in San Francisco was short of funds to distribute groceries to needy families. Oprah immediately sent a check for $50,000.

~

Oprah donates millions of dollars to back up her belief that knowing how to read and getting a good education are the keys to personal freedom

She gave $100,000 to the Harold Washington Library in Chicago, named in honor of the late Chicago mayor. The library opened in 1991.[36]

~

She has established many scholarship funds, including a $2 million grant to Morehouse College, a black men's liberal arts school in Atlanta; another $1 million to the science program at Spelman College, an historically black women's school; $1 million to a Chicago-area high school and $500,000 to a scholarship fund at the Henry

Homer Boys and Girls Club in Chicago. Additionally, Oprah has been spokesperson for A Better Chance, a privately funded organization that gives students from mainly inner-city schools the opportunity to attend the nation's best college preparatory and public schools. Proceeds from the *Oprah Winfrey: Make the Connection* go to A Better Chance.

∽

Regarding her donation to Atlanta's Morehouse College:

> *"I don't want it to go for paper clips. I want it to go to young African-American men."*[37]

Morehouse graduates include the Reverend Martin Luther King, Jr., Spike Lee, and Maynard Jackson, the first black mayor of Atlanta.

∽

Through her Angel Network, established in 1997, Oprah encourages others to become involved in volunteer work and charitable giving. Two of the first Angel Network programs were "Build an Oprah House" along with the Habitat for Humanity home construction program and "The World's Largest Piggy Bank" in which people were asked to donate their spare change to a scholarship fund for underprivileged kids.

In all, Habitat for Humanity has built more than 60,000 houses in 57 countries and expects to dedicate its 100,000th house in the year 2000.[38]

In 1998, 50 high school students across the country were granted $25,000 college scholarships. The Angel Network scholarships went to Youth of the Year for the Boys and Girls Clubs in each of the 50 states.[39]

Oprah's Angel Network has kindled all sorts of charitable partnerships, such as a Web site called "Shoes on the Net," which joined with *The Oprah Winfrey Show* in seeking Special Angels to donate footwear to those in need.[40]

> *"I started this because I believe people are ultimately good. I think television is a good way of opening people's hearts."* [41]

~

Oprah said that the tragic death of Diana, Princess of Wales, whom she once visited in London, inspired her to encourage everyday people to be more like Diana:

> *"You can reach out. You can be a princess, a queen in your own life by taking what you have and extending it to other people."*[42]

~

When Cher appeared on *The Oprah Winfrey Show* near Christmas, Oprah mentioned how difficult it was to find black angel ornaments and figurines. Soon she was inundated with so many that she pleaded with viewers to stop sending them. Oprah eventually donated her 571 black angels to the Angel Museum in Beloit, Wisconsin.[43]

~

But even Oprah can't please everyone, as this lament from the Jive-Turkey Web site demonstrates. The author says he used to love Oprah but now feels forsaken:

"Oprah has changed," wrote Jive Turkey. "She has decided to become a guru. Now she wants us to do nice things for others and to come on her show and talk about it, just because she tells us to. She's all 'random acts of kindness.' No way baby!

"The last thing I need when I'm watching afternoon TV is to feel guilty because I'm not loving my fellow human enough. I'm loving my couch and my snacks and my fifth cup of coffee. Isn't that enough?"[44]

ON ROMANCE

OH MEN!

> *"You know the old cliche, 'a good man is hard to find?'*
> *Well, it's true. And the smarter you get, the harder*
> *they are to find."*[1]

~

Oprah had several disappointing relationships in Nashville and Baltimore, and at one point even wrote a suicide note, she was so depressed over a breakup. One of the reasons Oprah was willing to leave Baltimore for Chicago is that she'd just ended a four-year affair with a married man and needed some distance to recover.

~

Oprah admits that in her youth:

> *"I was a doormat. But the thing about it is, you real-*
> *ize that there is a doormat overload out there because*
> *everybody's been one. Now I say 'I will never give up*
> *my power to another person.'"*[2]

~

Nowadays Oprah tells her on-air girlfriends what to do when men don't treat them right:

> *"You just pack your car and move out on him, you hear me?"[3]*

~

After moving to Chicago, Oprah went for a long time without romance in her life, but she had an image of the man she was looking for:

> *"He'd be taller than me, smarter than me, and not threatened by me. He'd have to be outgoing but know when to shut up. And I don't think it would matter if he was black, white or Chinese."[4]*

~

She finally found him. Oprah says her relationship with Stedman Graham is based on honesty:

> *"He is one person who would tell me the truth . . . and I would tell him the truth."[5]*

~

Graham says of Oprah: "I have helped her find her way in times of self-doubt, and for her part, she has certainly done the same for me. Each of us comes from a scarred family history. As someone who is given to constant self-analysis, she has opened herself up much sooner to the childhood traumas that haunted her into adulthood. It took me much longer to let the light in, and still, even now, I open the door to it little by little—one ray at a time."[6]

Among Oprah's favorite men friends is composer Quincy Jones. Jones discovered Oprah the actress when he was coproducing *The Color Purple*. Jones threw a 43rd birthday bash for Oprah at his home in the Bel-Air section of Los Angeles. Among the guests were filmmaker Steven Spielberg, actor Sidney Poitier, and Oprah's friend Gayle King. Patti Austin and Greg Philliganes entertained.[7]

~

Arnold Schwarzenegger, husband of Oprah's long-time friend Maria Schriver, is another man Oprah admires:

> *"Arnold is a mentor to a lot of men, but the thing that they're mentoring is the macho, the muscles. But what makes Arnold Arnold is the balance. He knows and practices sensitivity."*[8]

~

To Larry King, Oprah said:

> *"I love the fact that you love your daughter so much. I really do love that. Every time I talk to you, and in any conversation, wherever we are, wherever we meet, you always bring her up. I think that—I hope my dad does that about me."*[9]

~

Girlfriends introduce their single girlfriends to eligible guys, right? So does Oprah. While she was taping her show from Amarillo, Texas, Oprah covered the topic of eligible millionaires. Mike Mullen, a former pro football player, made his money in oil venture capital. After appearing on Oprah's show he received more than 20,000 letters, parcels, videotapes, and telephone calls. The post office where he maintains a box took the extra precaution of locking his application, with his home address on it, in the safe.[10]

ZIPPITY-DOO-DAH, OPRAH'S IN LOVE

Before she met her fiancé Stedman Graham, Oprah used to say:

> *"Mr. Right's coming, but he's in Africa and he's* walkin'.*"[11]*

~

She also used to say:

> *"My idea of heaven is a great big baked potato and someone to share it with."[12]*

Once she had Stedman to share with, she began to realize she didn't need all those potatoes.

~

About six months after she began dating Stedman, Oprah wasn't making any predictions about marriage, but she definitely was smitten:

> *"The success of my show is great, losing weight is great, but nothing compares with being in love. Zippity-doo-dah, I'm in* love!*"[13]*

He calls her "O" and she calls him "Steddy." Not long after they met, Oprah explained the attraction:

"He's kind, and he's supportive, and he's six-feet six-inches! He not only washes the dishes, he cooks."[14]

∼

Stedman seems to give Oprah the sense of emotional security that all people seek in their love life.

"Lots of people want to ride with you in the limo. But you want someone who'll help you catch the bus."[15]

∼

Not long after Oprah and Stedman became engaged, they set a sentimental date:

"We had set a wedding date that first year Stedman proposed. I was going to get married on September 8, which was the same day that my father and step-mother got married."[16]

∼

It's not clear why Oprah and Stedman have not yet wed. Some say Graham still resents being seen as Mr. Oprah Winfrey, although he wrote in his book, *You Can Make It Happen*, that he's overcome that annoyance. Some say it is because Oprah feels he rejected her when she was struggling with her weight problems. Still others insist Graham missed his chance by waiting too long to propose.[17] It is clear, however, that Oprah is weary of being asked when she plans to tie the knot.

> *"Neither of us is ready to get married and when we are, we'll get married."*[18]

~

> *"I am in no hurry to get married. I dislike this notion of a desperate woman who wants to get married. The only reason to get married is to have children, and I don't feel the urgency."*[19]

~

> *"Right now I'm in an independent, interdependent relationship, meaning that we support each other and offer a sense of strength for each other."*[20]

~

After years of agonizing over relationships and worrying that she would never marry, Oprah finally stopped putting pressure on herself:

> *"I no longer feel . . . that I have to have a man in order to make myself whole."*[21]

~

> *"I try to move with the flow of life and not dictate what life should be for me, but just let it flow."*[22]

~

If she decided to have children, though, Oprah would marry:

"I would never have children without the benefit of marriage. How could I speak before the thousands of teenagers I address each year and advise them not to bear children unless they are married?"[23]

~

When and if Oprah and Stedman marry, they will have the gift of free advice from one of America's best-known marriage counselors, Dr. Joyce Brothers. Dr. Brothers wrote about the pair several years back in her column in *Good Housekeeping*. She cautioned that couples who have been engaged or living together for a long time before getting married must do two things:

* First, they must have sincerely tried to solve their problems before marriage and

* Second, they must be determined to continue that work after the nuptials.

"Studies show that when two people live together but are not married," wrote Dr. Brothers, "there's an unspoken feeling between them that their relationship could be temporary. As a result, they often tend to gloss over their problems. Why make an issue, one or both may think, when we may not be together in a few years anyhow? Trouble can then occur when they do marry because they have not resolved problems and they may expect just saying 'I do' will work magic and all the problems will go away."[24]

Dr. Brothers added that Stedman seemed very affectionate and supportive and that Oprah would make a nurturing, loyal mother if the couple had children. The marriage, in short, had her blessing.

~ ✳ ~

OPRAH'S STEDDY

Oprah says that Stedman is "my rock."[25] He also has a corny-but-cute sense of humor. For one thing, he keeps telling the same old jokes.

"Every time we have artichokes for dinner, he goes, 'you might choke Artie, but you won't choke Stedman.' Every single time!"[26]

~

Stedman has even joked publicly about Oprah's weight problems. While making a speech, he referred to his girlfriend—"we've been through thick and thin—no pun intended."[27]

~

Stedman was a basketball star at Hardin-Simmons University in Abilene, Texas. He graduated in 1974, then went on to play with the European Basketball League. In 1979 Stedman earned a graduate degree in education from Ball State University in Muncie, Indiana.[28] He is divorced and has a grown daughter, Wendy. Wendy grew up living with her mother, Glenda, in Dallas but spent time with her father and Oprah.

Stedman worked in prison education before switching careers in the late 1980s.[29] He now owns a Chicago-based, sports-oriented marketing and public relations firm and is founder of a nonprofit organization called Athletes Against Drugs. Additionally, Stedman has written a column for *Inside Sports* magazine and is author of two inspirational books based on his life in sports.

"Sports is what I love," says Stedman.[30]

Stedman's first book, *You Can Make It Happen: A Nine Step Plan for Success*, was published by Simon & Schuster in 1997. A smaller book, *You Can Make It Happen Everyday*, was published by Fireside Books in 1998.

~

Graham is a globe-trotting businessman, but Oprah's friend Gayle King says he never has a roving eye:

"I'll even watch him sometimes," King says. "Somebody cute will walk by, and I'll go, 'I know he's gonna look!' and he never does! I think his thing is, 'When you have the best, why do you want to try other people?'"[31]

~

Stedman grew up in the working-class community of Whitesboro, New Jersey. He often heard the discouraging remark, "nothing good comes out of Whitesboro."[32]

He says he was too light-complexioned to be accepted by many blacks but not light enough to be accepted by most white people. Additionally, he was taunted by classmates because his two younger brothers were mentally disabled.

"I feel comfortable with who I am, although I haven't always," says Stedman. "I give Oprah credit for helping me understand that the source of my pain was in the past."[33]

~

Regarding Oprah's influence and wealth, he says:

"When you're with a powerful woman who makes more money than you—of course, she makes more money than everybody—it's tough on a man. But if you can build something for yourself that's special, it doesn't matter who your mate is."[34]

Stedman encourages economically disadvantaged people to focus on improving their lives and not to shrink from commercial success:

"We've got to get past the anger and start grabbing at opportunity," he explained in an article in which others criticized clothing manufacturers for capitalizing on black culture in youth fashions.

"There needs to be a bridge between corporate America and the African-American market, and the color to focus on is green, not black. Go get the money!"[35]

Oprah says of Stedman: "We get along so well because we want to do the same thing. We want to help people see their lives differently."[36]

Stedman apparently understand's Oprah's love for dogs. He gave her a puppy as a gift, and now she has more than a half-dozen dogs—some in Chicago, some at the farm. She's especially fond of Shane, a golden retriever:

"Shane's the king of our household. He gets whatever he wants and goes anywhere he wants. Except our bed. We love our dogs, but Stedman and I don't need company in bed."[37]

OPRAH
ON THE OUTSIDE

LIFE IS LIKE A MARATHON

Few of the thousands of runners and spectators at 1994 Washington, D.C., Marine Corps Marathon believed that racer No. 40 could ever finish the grueling, 26.2-mile race through the capitol mall, across the Potomac River and south to the Pentagon.

It was a personal triumph when Oprah Winfrey, who was never much of an athlete until she started running 18 months earlier, crossed the finish line. Of the 13,800 runners who entered the event, 4,240 dropped out. Despite a drizzling rain, Oprah averaged just over 10 minutes per mile and finished in 4 hours, 29 minutes, and 15 seconds.

"I was the girl to beat. One guy had a T-shirt on that said, 'I just want to beat Oprah.'"[1]

~

"Never did I feel I wasn't going to finish."[2]

~

Probably the highest praise for Oprah's full marathon came from a writer for *Running World*, the magazine for hardcore marathoners, who jogged near Oprah the entire time. She earned his respect for sticking to it, but the writer was equally impressed by the great affection the crowd showed for the talk show host. Oprah presented herself to the world that morning without makeup, without a glamorous hairdo, and, as the race progressed, dripping with sweat.

"Everyone's peering into the pack to find Oprah and cheering lustily when they spot her. These cheers are different than the high-pitched, explosive exhortations I've heard at major sports events. They are lower, longer, more profound, for Oprah is no superstar sports hero. She's just a formerly overweight woman chasing her dream and that's something everyone can relate to. 'WAY to go, OPRAH! You can DO it."[3]

"Life is a lot like a marathon. If you can finish a marathon, you can do anything you want."[4]

～

The book Oprah coauthored with her trainer Bob Greene, *Make the Connection: Ten Steps to a Better Body and a Better Life*, became a best-seller. Oprah describes her personal struggle with weight and shared her tips for living a healthy life. When the companion video *Oprah: Make the Connection* was released, she explained that her goal was to help people take control of their weight, their health, and their fitness:

"I am now about trying to convince people to stop wasting time. I know it's hard because it's much easier to want to believe there's some kind of magic [weight-loss] fix coming along. Just last year everybody believed that Redux and Fen-Phen were the magic fix."[5]

∼

"I don't believe that it's for everybody to be a size 8 or even a 12. I think you need to be where you physically feel the best for you."[6]

∼

Greene helped Oprah use her competitive nature to get fit. Oprah remembers her first, snaillike, 16-minute mile and the patronizing comments of fellow runners smugly urging her on as they dashed past:

"I'll never forget the day I passed them. Now, if Bob wants to push me, he'll say, 'See that woman in the pink suit? You can take her.' And I'll kill myself to run past her. I never realized how competitive I am. But I am. And I love to be underestimated."[7]

∼

Oprah rises early to run along Lake Michigan or to work out at the indoor track at Chicago's plush East Bank Club. She also lifts weights three days a week.

∼

After she slimmed down from a size 22 to a size 8, Oprah participated in a charity event to auction off 900 dresses and other items from her wardrobe.

"There was only one rack of 8s and 10s, and when I got there, there were only one or two items left," said *Pam Borchardt, a Chicago realtor. "People were grabbing armfuls as they went into the fitting room. Inside, people were trading clothes. I got a red Ungaro dress for $600. It still had a Marshall Field tag on it for $1,820."*[8]

～

Oprah's new style of dining was described in the best-selling *In the Kitchen with Rosie* by Oprah's chef Rosie Daley. Oprah now eliminates almost all fat from her diet, consumes at least two fruits and three vegetables daily, drinks at least eight glasses of water per day, limits or eliminates alcoholic beverages, and gradually reduces meal portions. Greene encourages people to have three meals plus two snacks per day, since healthful snacks will cut down hunger at mealtime.

A typical Rosie-inspired recipe: Simmer or steam vegetables in wine or low-sodium chicken broth and lightly sprinkle with Parmesan cheese. Delicious in a sandwich.[9]

～

Before she changed her diet, Oprah was an investor in the funky Chicago restaurant The Eccentric. One of the specialties on the menu was Oprah's own recipe for lumpy, garlic mashed potatoes, a most un-Rosie-like dish.

"Rosie's book and Oprah's restaurant have nothing to do with each other," explained Eccentric's chef, Jody

Denton. "In fact, since Oprah's been on a low-fat, low-salt, low-sugar diet, she hasn't been in the restaurant much herself."[10]

Perhaps it came as no surprise to Chicago diners when the restaurant closed in 1996.

～

Greene says he was impressed with Oprah's resolve from the first time he worked with her. He started her on a running program because it's the fastest way to drop weight. She began slimming down right away, then about three weeks into the program reversed and began to gain again, which Greene says is typical of a long-term weight-loss program. Some people use the weight gain as an excuse to quit, but Oprah didn't. As a result, her running time improved.

"She was so excited because she soon began seeing dramatic results," said Greene. "The body abides by the laws of physics. The more weight you lose, the faster you run. And the faster you run, the more weight you lose."[11]

～

Oprah's transition from a sedentary person to a marathon runner has allowed her to enjoy other physically demanding sports:

> *"I'm really hooked on skiing, and it's the first sport I'm pretty good at. But I'm not looking to be a champ, just adequate."*[12]

～

Greene says that people sometimes tell him "Oprah's got it easy because she has a personal chef and a personal trainer. But that's baloney. No one can run for you. She was on the track every morning. She worked herself as hard as any athlete I've seen. She deserves the results she achieved."[13]

～

Oprah says that will power comes from a determination to do something, but discipline comes from doing it. When you actually achieve your goal, you become powerful, she explains.

"Power is strength over time."[14]

FIGHTING FAILURE

For much of her adult life, Oprah has fought obesity. In 1988 she lost 67 pounds in about three months on Optifast, a liquid diet program for people who are at least 30 percent, or 50 pounds, above their healthy weight. She lost a pound a day while on the diet. It was then that Oprah realized some people didn't want her to win her battle with food.

One woman wrote a letter to the editor of *Newsday.* "As a fat woman, I have attempted 64 different diets. Oprah was meant to be fat. She fasted her way down to a size eight. Will the real Oprah Winfrey please come back to us!"[15]

The letter writer soon got her wish.

Like many of those using Optifast, Oprah quickly

regained the weight. Part of the problem, her love of corn chips, potato chips and especially potatoes:

"Any kind—french-fried, baked, boiled, hashed, au gratin, sliced or slivered ... mmmm!"[16]

~

"Some woman said to me, 'Well, at least we still have Barbara Bush,' and I thought, 'Oh, no, they don't like me any more.' I didn't deliberately go out and put the weight back on for that reason, but that concern was certainly embedded in my subconscious."[17]

~

Oprah confessed that she maintained her target weight of 145 pounds for only about 24 hours, partly because as soon as she lost the weight, she quit the program, rather than going on the transition and maintenance diet from Optifast to regular meals.

"I believed I was going to be among the 2 percent [who didn't regain the weight]. It pains me to say it, but I was wrong. I recently said to the universe, 'OK, take me, come on.' I'm ready."[18]

~

"Everybody's had those moments when you thought you were in control and then just lost it. And then something happens in your brain—You don't know what it is. You find yourself in the refrigerator attached to it."[19]

~

Oprah's weight was not a problem until she accepted a job anchoring the evening news in Baltimore. When producers of her show decided Oprah was too emotional in her delivery, they exiled her to a morning talk show:

"While interviewing a woman about the loss of her children and home in a fire, I cried, because it [the interview] was such an exploitive thing to have to do. And I apologized to the woman on the air."[20]

~

In an attempt to glamorize Oprah, her station management sent her to a chic French hairstylist in New York, who gave her a perm that caused her hair to fall out. Because she has a very large head, 24 ½ inches around, she could not find a wig to fit. Without realizing it, Oprah began overeating to make herself feel better.[21] Even so, her problems as a news anchor had a surprising resolution:

"They put me on the talk show just to get rid of me, but it was really my saving grace. The first day I did it, I thought, 'This is what I really should have been doing all along.'"[22]

~

Oprah realized later:

"I had no business anchoring the news in a major market. I was only 22."[23]

~

That insight didn't come immediately, however, and while she struggled to make the transition from a protected young woman living at home with her parents, working in a familiar town, to a larger, more visible, and much more demanding television job, she continued to comfort herself with food. Oprah was living in the Cross Keys residential community in Columbia, Maryland, across the street from a mall with a marvelous food court. On weekends she'd go from stall to stall, sometimes ordering something from every booth:

> *"I didn't realize at the time that by overeating I was trying to fill something deeper. The fact that I was lonely, somewhat depressed, and having a hard time adjusting to the new job never entered my mind."[24]*

~

Yet being overweight seldom worked against her. Oprah tested for the role of Sophia in the movie *The Color Purple*, then went on a diet and dropped 17 pounds. Director Steven Spielberg's office then called and offered her the role:

> *"They called me and said, 'You can't lose weight. Whatever you've lost, you'd better go out and find it.'"[25]*

~

Though her diets following the movie did not work for her, Oprah kept up the fight:

> *"I couldn't bear to think of myself as a quitter."[26]*

~

She attended a world championship boxing match where she was shocked to realize that she weighed the same as the 216-pound, former heavyweight champion Mike Tyson. Despite that, Oprah continued to gain and was 226 when she accepted her trophy at the 19th annual Emmy Awards. The shame she felt walking on stage that night prompted her to check into a health spa where she went to work on her weight problem.

> *"I think even with everything going on in my life, in my most loneliest moments and most frustrating moments, I felt I was the only person who had it this bad with weight. I felt like everyone else had been able to control their weight, but not me. There was something wrong with me. I think the video will be really helpful for people to see—everybody [overweight] feels the same way."*[27]

~

Although some fans felt sad about losing their rotund role model, plenty were cheering for Oprah to succeed in her battle to control her weight. When *Redbook* published a picture of the new, slimmer Oprah on its September 1995 cover, it was the magazine's hottest-selling issue of the year.[28]

~

Oprah realizes that there is a lesson in everything that happens, but even so, there were times she nearly gave up:

"Lots of times. Faith sustains me, though. Faith that, no matter what, no matter how difficult life becomes, I'll be okay."[29]

~

Oprah's movie, *Native Son*, based on the 1940 classic novel by Richard Wright, did not bring the acclaim of her first movie role, and the failure of her television series *Brewster Place* reportedly cost her $10 million, yet she has learned to deal with what others may consider failure:

"There is no such thing as failure in my life. I just don't believe in it. It's very easy to be where I am and always wonder how long it is going to last, instead of living in the moment. I have no fear of failure or of succeeding. I just do what I do and I know that will keep me in the best place."[30]

~

Oprah's persistence and self-confidence have been an inspiration to others. Where does that self-confidence come from?

"I think it just comes from living and taking notes while I'm living; appreciating the mistakes I've made, and looking at them as part of my growth."[31]

~

Confirming the notion of "once a foodaholic always a foodaholic," Oprah sometimes backslides under stress. During the time she was taping her TV show from

Texas following a full day in court, Oprah gained 11 pounds.

> *"I was strategizing with lawyers at night. I couldn't help but eat pie."[32]*

EMOTIONS AND HEALTH

Viewers enjoy *The Oprah Winfrey Show* partly because its vivacious host lays her feelings bare for all to see. Yet Oprah's emotionalism sometimes has caused trouble in her life, such as the time she lost the news-anchor job because she cried when covering tragic stories. So it comes as a shock to learn that *not* confronting her true feelings also has been a problem for Oprah.

> *"Everybody deals with their pain differently. Some become overachievers like me, and others become mothers who kill."[33]*

∽

> *"I used to brag, 'I don't ever get stress.' I'd ask, 'What is stress? What does it feel like?' The reason I didn't get stressed is, I ate my way through it."[34]*

∽

> *"I tell people 'You are responsible for your own life.' I take full responsibility for my successes or failures, from getting up and getting my own talk show to losing my luggage on a trip."[35]*

∽

"I could eat a feeling faster than anybody, put a little hot sauce on it and wouldn't recognize it until it showed up on my behind three days later."[36]

~

"I would have had this [weight] battle whether or not I was on TV. It happens to be the way I manifest my fears. To others it may be drugs or alcohol . . . the issue is not the food, it's what made you overeat in the first place."[37]

~

"My greatest failure was in believing that the weight issue was just about weight. It's not. It's about not being able to say no. It's about not handling stress properly. It's about sexual abuse. It's about all the things that cause other people to become alcoholics and drug addicts."[38]

~

"For me, food was comfort, pleasure, love, a friend, everything. I consciously work every day at not letting food be a substitute for my emotions."[39]

~

"What I've learned about being angry with people is that it generally hurts you more than it hurts them. All the anger that you're trying to vent breeds so much frustration."[40]

~

"If you're angry, be angry and deal with it. Don't go eat a bag of Ruffles."[41]

Bob Greene helped Winfrey get in touch with her emotional self, often by asking questions that help her get to the heart of a matter. Once while they were on a walk, the fitness trainer asked Oprah how often she experienced real joy.

Her most joyous time, she recalled, was while filming the movie *The Color Purple*. It "was the first time I ever remember being in a family of people where I truly felt loved."[42]

"It was a spiritual evolvement for me. I learned to love people doing that film."[43]

Since then, Oprah has worked harder at understanding the nature of love and how to give, accept, and recognize love.

Accepting love is not always easy for those who were abused or neglected as children.

"I don't receive love as well as I give it. Actually, I don't receive anything as well as I give it."[44]

As her life illustrates, Oprah does best when she honors her feelings:

"Gut is what got me where I am today."[45]

Although she is learning to confront her feelings, Oprah still believes in taking responsibility for them.

Over and over again, she tells her fans to find strength in themselves, seek the truth, and don't give your life to another:

"If you are struggling, you can't blame the Better Business Bureau. You can't blame your mother. You can't blame George Bush."[46]

~ ✳ ~

THE WOMAN WHO CRIED

Back in the 1980s there was a French film entitled *The Woman Who Cried*. The heroine sobbed and sobbed and sobbed, but she was no Oprah Winfrey. Winfrey sometimes insists that she isn't a crier, but her fans know better. She's the kind of woman you like to boo-hoo along with. Understandably, she cried on television when talking about being sexually abused as a child and again when confessing to having used cocaine. These were painful revelations. But like the rest of us, Oprah sniffles when talking about subjects that are nostalgic, romantic, and just too wonderful to bear without happy tears.

Oprah did a show on teachers who have had a deep influence on their pupils and she invited her fourth-grade teacher, Mrs. Duncan. It was the first time Oprah realized that Mrs. Duncan had a full name:

"You know, your teachers never had names. I said, sobbing, 'Her name's Mary!' I couldn't believe it."[47]

~

Before Oprah created Harpo Entertainment and gained control of her empire, seven of her staff members were refused raises by the station management. To compensate Oprah gave each staffer a Christmas gift of $10,000 in cash, stuffed inside rolls of toilet paper:

> *"It was great. Everybody wept and had a wonderful time. It feels good to be able to do things like that with no strings attached, just because I can."*[48]

Nothing like a heart tugging romance novel such as *The Bridges of Madison County* to bring out the tissues:

> *"Read* Bridges *in an afternoon, sitting in my living room and crying."*[49]

Wouldn't you know it? When Oprah was filming *The Color Purple*, she says the most difficult scene for her was the one in which she had to cry.

BEAUTY

When in 1986 Oprah Winfrey became the first African American female anchor at WJZ-TV in Baltimore, she didn't conform to the beauty standards for the typical female newscaster. She remembers her bosses telling her:

"We think your hair is too thick, your eyes are too far apart, and your nose is too wide."

After a disastrous visit to a New York salon that was supposed to make her more comely, Oprah recalls:

"I had two little spriggles, like a bald man. My sense of beauty was shot completely."[50]

~

It took courage to continue when everything seemed to go wrong on the job.

"You come to learn a lot about yourself when you're bald and black and an anchorwoman in Baltimore."[51]

~

Some of Oprah's conviction that she wasn't beautiful came from the image of beauty that prevailed when she was a child. She was a "fudge brownie" in a world that favored "gingerbreads" and "vanilla creams."[52]

". . . I felt really ugly because the lighter your complexion, the prettier you were. My half-sister was lighter and she got all the attention and I thought it was because she was the prettiest. I was the smartest, but no one praised me for being smart."[53]

~

Oprah has saucer-size amber-colored eyes—or hazel when she wears colored contact lenses. Those large, expressive eyes plus her wide smile make her very photogenic. Even as a little girl she had a larger than normal head, and her big hairdos make her an even larger presence, both on television and in person. Oprah is five-feet six-inches tall, when things are going well, she weighs around 150 pounds, and she wears size 10 shoes. Although she won Miss Black

Tennessee as a teen, Oprah has trouble seeing herself as a beauty. "It's a compliment I can't take," she said in 1986.[54]

~

Negative feelings about her body were reinforced when *TV Guide* magazine ran a cover shot of Oprah, singling her out as the richest woman on television. She was pictured in a gauzy dress sitting atop a pile of money. Not only had Oprah not posed on a heap of money, she hadn't worn the gauzy dress—in fact, she hadn't worn the body. The photo was a composite of Oprah Winfrey's face attached to Ann-Margret's torso. A shocked Ann-Margret had no trouble identifying the 10-year-old photograph. The hand was wearing her ring.

"Oprah would not pose on a pile of money like that," insisted her spokeswoman, "nor would she pose in that revealing a dress."[55]

~

Oprah's talk show host–buddy Gayle King says that being on television certainly makes *her* feel prettier.

She comes to work fresh out of the shower with wet hair, still wearing shower shoes. The hairdresser and makeup artist get busy. "They wave a little magic wand and I look like the girl on the cover of the magazine. It's fabulous."[56]

~

By having a personal trainer, makeup artist, hair-dresser, and fashion advisor, surely Oprah's self-image has improved. Losing weight helped:

> *"There are a few problems I don't have, like those women who lose weight and still think they are fat. I've never had that. I'm looking at myself as a size eight, and I'm thinking, I'm pretty cute!"*[57]

Back in 1988, Oprah explained her view of herself:

> *"I don't see myself as pretty. The word 'beautiful' isn't even in my vocabulary. It doesn't mean I don't love myself, but I do know what I am. I'm a wonderful, bright, loving person, but I am not beautiful."*[58]

Certainly the image of Oprah as a beautiful woman has been confirmed by the media in recent years.

Revlon featured Oprah in a series of "unforgettable woman" advertisements, including one in a form-fitting leopard print dress. In 1997 she was chosen by *People* magazine as one of the 50 Most Beautiful People in the World.

The repentant *TV Guide* named Oprah one of the best-dressed people on television. "In her ten years on national television," said the magazine, "Winfrey's look has consistently and fabulously evolved from an '80s gloss to a '90s sheen. Gone are the jewel-tone frocks, the colossal collars, and that catsuit for her Revlon ad. In their place is a more subtle, more subdued sensibility."

And, wrote *TV Guide*, when Oprah wants to party, she knows what to wear. "Remember her showstopping Gianfranco Ferre gown at last year's Academy Awards, or her shining silver Richard Tyler suit at the Daytime Emmys?" What the magazine editors said they'd really like to see, though, is a regal wedding gown. Now, that would sell magazines.[59]

OPRAH
ON THE INSIDE

GOD, THE FORCE WITHIN US

Oprah sometimes recites this verse from the Epistle to the Ephesians, chapter 4, verse 6. "One God and father of all, who is above all, and through all, and in you all."

~

"There's only one way I've been able to survive being raped, molested, whipped, rejected . . . only one way to cope with fears of pregnancy, my mother on welfare, my being fat and unpopular. As corny as this sounds, my faith in God got me through."[1]

~

"There have been times in my life when I was absolutely devastated: colored girl raised in Mississippi, anchoring the news in Baltimore, Maryland, and went to get a perm. All of my hair fell out, ended up bald on the news—devastated. Thought my life was over. It was really just the beginning because God had dreamed a bigger dream for me than I had for myself."[2]

"I am guided by a higher calling. It's not so much a voice as it is a feeling. If it doesn't feel right to me, I don't do it."[3]

～

"When I'm feeling real bad, I put on Aretha Franklin's album Amazing Grace *and I grab my Bible. I ask myself, 'Oprah, are you going to be a victim, or are you going to take charge of your life?' And when I'm in control, I feel like soaring over the mountains. I move with the flow and take life's cures, letting the universe handle the details. I know exactly where I'm going. And God's right beside me all the way."*[4]

～

"It is not being born again. It's an evolution, a realization of how life works—meaning that God is the center of the universe. Once you understand that, it's all really very simple."[5]

～

"I remember when I was four, watching my Grandma boil clothes in a huge iron pot. I was crying and Grandma asked, 'What the matter with you, girl?' 'Big Mammy,' I sobbed, 'I'm going to die someday.' 'Honey,' she said, "God doesn't mess with His children. You gotta do a lot of work in your life and not be afraid. The strong have got to take care of the others.'

"I soon came to realize that my grandma was loosely translating from the Epistle to the Romans

*in the New Testament—'We that are strong ought to
bear the infirmities of the weak.' Despite my age, I
somehow grasped the concept. I knew I was going to
help people, that I had a higher calling, so to speak."[6]*

~

Oprah was raised in the Baptist Church, but now:

*"I have church with myself: I have church walking
down the street. I believe in the God force that lives
inside all of us, and once you tap into that, you can
do anything."[7]*

She also reads the Christian booklet, *The Daily Word*.
When Oprah does go to church, she attends Trinity
United Church of Christ on Chicago's South Side.[8]

~

Oprah is tolerant of other people's style of religious
worship: Why?

*"Well, each person gets God at whatever level they're
able to acccept."[9]*

~

Does Oprah herself ever feel godlike in the way that
she changes people's lives? Not at all:

*"Because I'm so connected to the bigger picture of
what God is, I realize I'm just a particle in the God
chain. I see God as the ocean, and I'm a cup of water
from the ocean."[10]*

~

"I am not God . . . I hope I don't give that impression. I am not God. I keep telling Shirley MacLaine, 'You can't go around telling people you are God.' It's a very difficult concept to accept."[11]

SPIRITUAL GROWTH

"I understand that many people are victimized, and some people certainly more horribly than I have been. But you have to be responsible for claiming your own victories, you really do. If you live in the past and allow the past to define who you are then you never grow."[12]

~

"If people want to solve their problems they must sooner or later reach inward to bring about a positive difference in their lives."[13]

~

"Everything that happens to you happens for a reason—everything you do in your life comes back to you. I call it 'Divine Reciprocity.' That's why I try to be kind to people—more for my sake than theirs."[14]

~

"I do everything to the absolute ultimate. I grow until I can't grow any more in a certain position. And then another door opens for me. . . . I can't stand to be bored."[15]

~

After withdrawing her memoirs from her publisher, Oprah said she wasn't ready to write about herself, since she was in the midst of a major growth spurt:

"I am a woman in progress. I'm just trying like everyone else. I try to take every conflict, every experience and learn from it. All I know is that I can't be anybody else. And it's taken me a long time to realize that."[16]

"I'm just taking a day at a time. That's the difference between myself now and four or five years ago. I live in the moment."[17]

"I believe people must grow and change; they must, or they will shrivel up. Their souls will shrink. I hope always to be expanding my life, always to be expanding my thinking. I want to expand myself in all ways," Oprah pauses, and then laughs, *"except the physical."[18]*

When *The Oprah Winfrey Show* entered its 12th season on the air, Oprah set a goal for the program:

"I want people to have the grandest vision for their lives."[19]

What about her own grand vision?

"I ask that I be able to live my life so that it magnifies the power of God that is in me. I need to get to

the point where I have as much love in my heart for
other people as I should have. And I'm striving for
wisdom, truth and love."[20]

SPIRITUAL TEACHERS

Gurus are there "not to teach us about their divinity but to teach us about our own."[21]

~

Her personal trainer, Bob Greene, has served as both Oprah's philosopher and psychologist:

"Having to face the truth of myself. I can be working
out and he'll slam me with one of those life questions
that just knocks me to my knees."[22]

~

Maya Angelou taught Oprah to listen to her inner voice:

"Maya tells me all the time, if you're going to look
inside yourself you have to be quiet and listen."[23]

~

That inner voice often tells Oprah when to move from one stage of development to the next:

"When you have finished growing in one place or
time, you know. Your soul tells you when it's time to
move on."[24]

~

Oprah gives credit to Stedman Graham for helping her deal with personal growth. In one of his books on success, Graham writes, "Learn to celebrate your successes and acknowledge your defeats, but then move on to the next opportunity and challenge."[25]

~

Oprah herself has become a spiritual teacher:

> *"I feel that my show is a ministry; we just don't take up a collection. And I feel that it is a teaching tool, without preaching to people about it. That's my intent."*[26]

~ ✳ ~

OPRAH'S FAVORITE BIBLE PASSAGES

Reading the Bible each day has been a lifetime habit. Oprah Winfrey has at least four of them, one each in her office, car, Chicago apartment, and her Indiana farm. By reading the Bible, Oprah finds:

> *"Every answer to every question that man could ever pose has already been answered."*[27]

~

> *"I read it all the time. It just calms me, gives me peace."*[28]

~

Oprah's favorite verse is from Paul's epistle to the Philippians:

Philippians 3:14: "I press toward the mark for the prize of the high calling of God in Jesus Christ."

~

Oprah's grandmother taught her to be compassionate by referring to this verse:

Romans 15:1: "We then that are strong ought to bear the infirmities of the weak, and not to please ourselves."

~

She also enjoys reading the fourth chapter of Epistle to the Ephesians, which ends this way:

Ephesians 4: 31: "Let all bitterness, and wrath, and anger, and clamor, and evil speaking, be put away from you with all malice. And be yet kind to one another, tenderhearted, forgiving one another, even as God for Christ' s sake hath forgiven you."

~ ✳ ~

OPRAH ON PRAYER

"My prayer to God every morning on my knees is that the power that is in the universe should use my life as a vessel, or a vehicle, for its work. Prayer. That's the central thing for me."[29]

~

"God blesses you better when you pray on your knees."[30]

~

"Last year I asked [God] for freedom. Did I not come out of myself in a big way, breaking out of that fat shell? And this year I asked for clarity. I have become more clear about my purpose in television and this show."[31]

~

"I act as if everything depends upon me and pray as if everything depends on God."[32]

~

In prayers we speak to God, but it also is important to listen for God's response:

". . . what I try to do is get God on the whisper. He always whispers first. Try to get the whisper before the earthquake comes because the whisper is always followed by a little louder voice, then you get a brick I say, and then sometimes a brick wall, and then the earthquake comes. Try to get it on the whisper."[33]

ON TRUTH
AND COURAGE

THE CURE FOR FEAR

"I have a lot of things to prove to myself. One is that I can live my life fearlessly. But I don't have anything to prove to the world."[1]

~

When Oprah was sued by Texas cattle ranchers over a show in which she publicly swore off eating hamburgers, she decided not to settle out of court. She went to Texas for the trial, even though she was frightened of how she might be treated in a city that at first seemed hostile to her:

"Because the true test of courage is to be afraid and to go ahead and to do it anyway. To be scared, to have your knees knocking, but to walk on in there anyway."[2]

NOTE: For more about what happened, see "The Cow Row" and "The Amarillo Victory."

~

"More than anything else, I would call myself a truth seeker. I'm always looking for truth and its value in my life."[3]

~

"I think the ones who survive in life do it by hammering at it one day at a time. You do what you have to do to get through today, and that puts you in the best place tomorrow."[4]

~

Little things in Oprah's life take bravery too:

"The other night I roasted a whole chicken [for Stedman] and had to watch him eat it while I ate my green beans. But I can take it. I'm a big girl."[5]

~

When Oprah needs more courage, she can turn to Stedman for inspiration. In one of his books on leadership Graham says, "We all have fears. Fears are real only when we make them real by investing too much in them. When we allow fear to dominate our lives, we give it too much power. The only real cure for fear is faith and courage."[6]

~ ✳ ~

THE TRUTH WILL SAVE YOU

Patrice Gains, a *Washington Post* reporter, was Oprah Winfrey's guest on January 13, 1995 to discuss her book about her own experience with middle-class drug use, *Laughing in the Dark*. But the show took a surprising turn.

Oprah stood before the audience and confessed her own "great shame." Twenty years earlier she had used crack cocaine, hoping the shared experience would bring her closer to a man she was dating.

"I was so in love with him I would have done anything for him," she said.

When the camera cut to a commercial, Oprah, 41, put her microphone aside and sat on the edge of the stage weeping.[7]

~

The confession, Oprah said, was the most difficult thing she's ever said:

> *"It's my life's great big secret. It was such a secret because—I realize [with] the public person I have become—if the story ever were revealed, the tabloids would exploit it and what a big issue it would be."*[8]

The revelation was covered widely in the media, from the tabloids to *Time* magazine, but the fact that Oprah told the story herself and expressed her remorse stripped away the gossip value.[9]

~

Oprah's drug use occurred between 1973 and 1976 while she was anchoring a television news show in Nashville.

> *"I had a perfect round little Afro. I went to church every Sunday . . . and I did drugs."*[10]

~

"I would have felt like a hypocrite, not saying [I had smoked cocaine], talking to people about baring their souls and standing there like I didn't know what they were talking about. When Charmaine [a cocaine user] said 'I want to come here because I knew you would be honest and straightforward with me,' I knew I had to say something.

"My heart was beating fast. I could see the tabloids before me. But I would have felt like a fraud if I hadn't said it."[11]

~

"It threw me completely off guard," said Kim Davis, a seven-months-pregnant recovering addict who also appeared on the show. "You would never dream she had a problem with drugs."

Davis continued, "She said she was involved with a man and she did drugs when she was with him.... When he was gone the drugs were gone. It was weird. I just saw this woman I've admired so much. And she's been where I've been and she pulled out of it. I'm 35 and I've done nothing for most of my life but get high. She got away from it. It gave me hope."[12]

~

"I shared this with Maya Angelou ... and you know what she said to me? It really turned my life around and I say this to you. 'You did then what you knew how to do and when you knew better you did better.' And I'll never forget that."[13]

~

"What I learned from it, is the thing that you fear the most truly has no power. Your fear of it is what has the

power. But the thing itself cannot touch you. What I learned that day is that the truth really will set you free."[14]

"Just tell the truth. It'll save you every time."[15]

ON DOING RIGHT

GOOD WORK

". . . part of the reason why I am as successful as I have been, [is] because success wasn't the goal. The process was. I wanted to do good work."[1]

~

"I always feel if you do right, right will follow."[2]

~

"I believe we are all given the power to use our lives as instruments. What we think is what manifests in reality for all of us. If all of us would only strive for excellence in our own backyards, we would bring that excellence to the rest of the world. Yes, we would."[3]

~

"Whatever good you put out in the universe [will] come back, and whatever bad you put out [will] come back as well."[4]

~

When Oprah went to Texas to defend her show about the possibility of mad cow disease in the United States, it wasn't her first time in court.

She reported to jury duty in 1993 at the Chicago federal courthouse. "My name is Oprah Winfrey. I have a talk show. I am single. I have eight dogs—five golden retrievers, two black labs, and a mongrel," she told the judge.

"I'm just doing my civic duty, even though I was planning on going skiing," she told reporters.[5]

~

Striving to do good work is worth the effort:

"In the end, all you have is your reputation."[6]

THE COW ROW

"This isn't George Bush saying 'I don't like broccoli,'" insisted Emory University Professor David J. Bederman. No, it was much bigger. This was Oprah Winfrey, heard worldwide, saying that she wouldn't be eating hamburgers any time soon.[7]

The controversy exploded when guest Howard Lyman, head of the Humane Society's "Eating with Conscience" campaign, described cattle feeding procedures in the United States that, conceivably, could lead to the spread of the dreaded bovine spongiform encephalopathy (BSE), or mad cow disease. In Great Britain, Creuzfeldt-Jakob disease, a human brain illness, had killed ten people, and health authorities there had shown a link between Creuzfeldt-Jakob in humans and BSE in cows.

Although there are no confirmed cases of either mad cow disease or Creuzfeldt-Jakob disease in the United States, Lyman told Oprah that the risk existed because of the practice of feeding cattle the carcasses of other cows that had died from unknown causes.

"It has just stopped me cold from eating another hamburger," Oprah blurted out.[8]

Texas cattle rancher Paul Engler claimed that Oprah's show sent beef prices into a downward spiral and cost the cattle industry millions of dollars. Indeed, after the show, cattle prices plummeted and kept falling for two weeks in what beef traders called the "Oprah Crash" of 1996. Some experts claimed that Oprah's statements were incidental since meat prices already were in decline.

~

Oprah followed up with a second show on beef-borne illness on April 23, 1996. During that show, Dr. Gary Weber of the National Cattlemen's Beef Association (NCBA) and Iowa cattle rancher Connie Greig assured viewers that the cattle industry works hard to produce a safe and wholesome food. The NCBA said it has tracked the bovine spongiform encephalopathy problem for 11 years in an effort to make sure BSE does not infect the U.S. cattle population.[9]

Ranchers were not appeased by the second show.

Bill O'Brien, co-owner of Texas Beef Group and one of the several cattlemen that sued, said it was too little, too late. "She didn't go on that program and eat a hamburger before the world."[10]

In Texas, it is against the law to say untrue things about meat or other food products. A group of ranchers, Engler among them, sued Winfrey, demanding $12 million in damages.

Although she was worried about her personal safety and concerned that she would not be able to maintain the quality of her shows during a long trial, in 1997 Oprah decided against seeking an out-of-court settlement. She would go to Texas to fight the charges because she felt an obligation to defend free speech.

"I come from a people who struggled and died to use their voice in this country and I refuse to be muzzled."[11]

~

"And after all, I—I never forget that I am an African-American woman going into Texas and all that has meant in our history. I was afraid of that. I was afraid that I would not be able to find a—a jury of my peers who would be able to understand, first of all, television and what I was trying to say on television."[12]

~

"When I told them [the Harpo production team], they were looking at me literally like stunned deer.

But I have the best team in TV, and they started to work and began brainstorming. They all rose to the occasion, but they rose slowly."[13]

~

Despite Oprah's worries, there were early clues that Texans would treat her well. One Texas headline writer playfully dubbed the trial and the surrounding media circus "Beauty and the Beef."[14]

Even cattle ranchers were not united in their criticism of Oprah. One group of beef producers posted an "Open Letter to Oprah Winfrey" on the Internet saying that they were dedicated to producing high-caliber food, but there were problems with the quality of meat in America. They called for inspection and labeling of imported beef that often is mixed with U.S. inspected beef to make hamburger.[15]

~

On the witness stand, Oprah explained that her show is not a news show. Rather it is based on discussions in which guests are free to express their opinions, and while the producers instruct guests to be honest, they are free to tell the truth as they know it:

"I personally have the responsibility to tell the truth. But truth in real life or TV is not necessarily the truth in a court of law. There are myriad ways to interpret an event or an experience. You can tell the truth without having to tell the whole truth. And we believe in the truth, Mr. Coyne."[16]

Joe Coyne is the attorney who represented the cattle producers in court.

～

Will Hueston, a former U.S. Department of Agriculture spokesman, had been a guest on the original show, but his statements in defense of safe beef were cut to just a few seconds. Hueston said he felt "ambushed" when he appeared on the show. That day on the set, he said, Oprah was a little testy. "She snapped orders and appeared to be in a bad mood."[17]

Later Hueston behaved on the witness stand just like a guest on Oprah's show. He began to cry, apologizing for saying that the mad cow show created a "lynch mob mentality."[18]

～

After nearly a month in court, Oprah was found innocent of causing a crash in the beef market. She broke into tears. Outside the courtroom she thrust her right fist into the air victoriously:

"Yes!
"Free speech not only lives, it rocks."[19]

～

"It was the most trying, but also most validating experience I've ever had. Every day [in the court] one of the bailiffs would say, 'God bless these United States and this honorable court' and I feel the same. I think the system works."[20]

Juror Pat Gowdy said after the verdict: "We felt that a lot of rights have eroded in this country. Our freedom of speech may be the only one we have left to regain what we lost."[21]

Coyne claimed that Oprah's celebrity status had influenced the trial's outcome. "You'd have to be blind to say [jurors] weren't influenced by one of the 25 most influential Americans."[22]

David J. Bederman, an Emory University law professor who tried to overturn Georgia's food product disparagement law in 1995, disagreed. The "beef beef" was a serious legal test case for the new type of law that had been passed in several states.

"However you cut it, the Texas cattlemen have been held to traditional constitutional proofs, and they failed," said Bederman. "They carefully picked this venue and jury and—even in the heart of Texas beef country—Oprah still whupped them."[23]

After Oprah's court victory, *Time* magazine wrote, "The winner Oprah. She's the most powerful woman in the United States. Laws be damned."[24]

This may not be the final word on the case. A group of Texas cattle feeders filed another similar suit in state court, and that case is pending.[25] Furthermore, Paul Engler appealed the Amarillo decision in the U.S. 5th Circuit Court of Appeals in New Orleans, charging that the judge made incorrect rulings and other errors. That case is pending as well.

～

Oprah expressed special pride in the way she, her lawyers, and her staff handled the Amarillo experience:

> *"We took what was given to us. It was a big old fat lemon. And we didn't make lemonade out of it, we made a lemon pound cake."*[26]

THE AMARILLO VICTORY

At first it looked as if just being in Amarillo would be a nightmare for Oprah Winfrey:

> *"I was scared to come here at first. I saw where there were bumper stickers that said, 'The Only Mad Cow in Texas Is Oprah.' That hurt my feelings."*[27]

～

When word spread that Oprah was coming to town, Chamber of Commerce President Gary Molberg sent his staff a memo saying "We are not going to have any red-carpet roll-outs, key to the city, flowers . . .

sent to her or her production company, and no chamber employees are to be at her show if she has them in Amarillo." Molberg said the chamber would provide any information Winfrey requested, "but the Amarillo Chamber of Commerce fully supports the cattle feeder industry because they are a vital part of Amarillo."[28]

Molberg's attitude may have been predictable, since Amarillo was founded in 1876 by a rancher who went there to take advantage of the miles and miles of grasslands. About 150 cattle feedlots do business in the Texas Panhandle today, and Amarillo's largest corporate employer is Iowa Beef Processors, a slaughterhouse that is workplace to 3,300 people.[29]

~

In addition to the emotional strain, her time in Amarillo was physically exhausting for Oprah. She rose at 5:30 A.M. to work out, spent from 9:00 A.M. until 5:00 P.M. in court. She then went to the Amarillo Little Theater, where she taped her show from 7:00 until 8:30 P.M. After the taping, Oprah spent hours with her lawyers preparing for the next day in court.[30]

She took up residence at the Ataberry Bed & Breakfast and began working out at the Downtown Athletic Club. As it turned out, Texans treated their temporary citizen nicely. One Amarillo resident was among the lunch-hour spectators at the trial. "We love you bad girl. Go girl!" she called to Oprah.[31]

The celebrity guests who flew into town to be on Oprah's show thrilled Amarillo residents. They included John Travolta and Kathy Bates from the movie *Primary Colors*; country-western singer Clint Black and his wife, Lisa Hartman Black; the teenage singing sensation LeAnn Rimes; country-western singer Kenny Rogers; and action-adventure actor Chuck Norris.

At one point Maya Angelou arrived and sat quietly in the packed courtroom. "I am here to lift Oprah up," explained Angelou. "For that and no other reason."[32]

~

Not only did Oprah win the lawsuit, in the end she won the hearts of cow-eating Texans to such an extent that the "mad cow" bumper stickers on pickup trucks gave way to "Amarillo Loves Oprah" signs. A crowd turned up at her hotel on January 29 to serenade Oprah on her 44th birthday. The day also was brightened by a visit from boyfriend Stedman Graham.

Although she was tuckered out by the experience and glad to get home to Chicago, Oprah said there were many pleasant things about the time she spent in Amarillo:

"I think I've come through a much stronger person."[33]

~

"*I am grateful for the kindness of strangers. I'll miss Amarillo. I'll miss the sunsets and the sunrises. I've been fortunate to see some of the most beautiful sunrises I've ever seen in my life.*"[34]

ON SOLVING THE WORLD'S PROBLEMS

A PASSION FOR CHILDREN'S RIGHTS

"If I could change just one thing, I would stop people from beating their kids. Not just beating, but molesting kids, verbally abusing kids, neglecting kids. The dishonor of children is the single worst problem in this country. If we ended it, there would be an incredible ripple effect on society. From the thousands of shows I have done over the past 10 years, I see that the way people were treated as children causes them to grow up and behave certain ways as adults. I see it as the root of almost every problem in our society."[1]

～

During 1990, The Year of the Child, Oprah Winfrey devoted at least one show each month to children's issues.

"What stops the cycle of abuse is awareness."[2]

～

In 1991 Oprah initiated the National Child Protection Act and testified before the U.S. Senate to encourage members to pass a law establishing a national database of all convicted child abusers. In 1993 Winfrey watched as President Clinton signed the national "Oprah bill" into law.

At her testimony, Oprah said:

> *"You lose your childhood when you've been abused. My heart goes out to those children who are abused at home and have no one to turn to."[3]*

~

Harper's Bazaar magazine asked Oprah to name her Christmas wish:

> *"My wish is that children be treated as people, and not as property; that their rights as human beings on the planet, to food, shelter, education and health, be taken seriously."[4]*

~

Oprah Winfrey has taken up both popular and unpopular battles, including a stand against guns:

> *"There are just too many guns lying around that kids can get their hands on. There is no reason 15 children should be dying every day as the result of guns."[5]*

~

After meeting Kalvin, a 13-year-old living in the Westside Chicago projects whom she considered taking into her own home until boyfriend Stedman pointed out that Oprah would have to take in Kalvin's whole family, Oprah started a program called Families for a Better Life. Kalvin's family became the pilot project in a $6 million program that helps welfare families improve their situations. Oprah tutored Kalvin, paid for school supplies, while Kalvin's mother earned her GED and eventually was able to move her family out of the projects to a safe home.

> *"I have always believed that you help people one at a time. That's how lives are changed."*[6]

Kalvin's mother says her problems are still a long way from over. She works long hours and her children miss their old friends, but at least she now has hope for their future.

Gordon Johnson of the Jane Addams Hull House Association, which ran the Better Life program, says that the remarkable part is that Oprah spends time with the families. "We may not all have $6 million to offer. But we have time and energy. If Oprah Winfrey can make time to jump into a project like this, any of us can."[7]

~

Oprah showed her television audience a ring that had been sent to her by Steven Spielberg, director of the movie *The Color Purple*:

> *"He wrote me a note saying that every day on the show I try to save the entire world. And engraved in*

this ring is a quote from Schindler's List. *'Whoever saves one life saves the entire world.'"*[8]

Later in the same show Oprah added:

"That's really what I try to do in my life—try to reach out and save other people."[9]

WHY OPRAH SELDOM WATCHES TELEVISION

"It promotes false values."[10]

~

"I saw a show where there was an entire row of black men and the caption beneath their names was 'Men Who Know They Are Dogs' and there was not a white face among them. When I see producers bring on black people in such a way that they fulfill every negative stereotype we have ever seen or heard, I am embarrassed for us."[11]

~

There is a big exception to Oprah's dislike of television—she enjoys *The Andy Griffith Show* and often watches reruns while working out on the treadmill. "I've seen every one now. I'm repeating the Best of Barney."[12]

However, she'd like one change to the little town of Mayberry. "If we could just have one little black neighbor down the street. . . ."[13]

Griffith participated in a salute to Oprah when she won a Lifetime Achievement award at the 1998 Daytime Emmys. "I understand you're a fan of the old Griffith shows," said Andy. "I want you to know I'm a fan of yours."[14]

MAKING TV BETTER

Several years ago Oprah realized how tawdry TV talk shows had become and she was disgusted. No wonder critics began to called them the "nuts and sluts" shows.

"There's no honor, no integrity in it."[15]

∽

In a speech to television industry executives, Oprah implored:

"Let's abandon the 'if it bleeds, it leads' news philosophy of the past. Enough of the body bags, ballistic tests, and bizarre crime scenes. If you repeat a problem, the problem only gets repeated.

"We really ought to ask ourselves, 'Do we want our children to spend hours viewing the images we're putting on the tube these days? Do we want our children influenced by visions of earth and destruction, carnages and car crashes, sex and scandals?"[16]

∽

Oprah strives to make her show a positive influence:

"I've been guilty of doing trash TV and not even thinking it was trash. I don't want to do it anymore. But for the past four years we've been leading the way for doing issues that change people's lives. So I'm irritated and frustrated at being lumped in with the other shows. I think I'm blamed for it all. There was an article on the Oprahization of America, lumping me and O.J. going down the freeway in the same category. I'm thinking, 'what is he talking about?'"[17]

~

"What we're really doing is trying to disassociate ourselves from the 'trash pack.' There's a whole genre of television talk shows that I'm not proud to be a part of and don't appreciate being lumped in with. So, I have made a real effort to do talk shows that are more responsible, shows that are going to be a benefit and not belittle people."[18]

~

"I cannot listen to other people blaming their mothers for another year. We're not gonna book a show where someone is talking about their victimization."[19]

~

Oprah continues to make headlines for her celebrity guests, but she also has hosted shows about what to do in an emergency, finding lost relatives, deadbeat dads, Native American anger, and mothers who fight to protect their children from drugs and violence.[20]

Although she vowed to lift the standard of her show, Oprah insists that her show never fell to the depths of bad taste and poor judgment that some of her competitors did:

> *"From the beginning, my philosophy has been that people deserve to come and to leave [my show] with their dignity. I never did what you see on the air today—nowhere close to it—because I never wanted people to be humiliated and embarrassed. And that is why I will not accept any kind of responsibility for the crap that we see on TV everyday."*[21]

∽

> *". . . a good talk show will stimulate thought, present new ideas, and maybe give you a sense of hope where there wasn't any—a feeling of encouragement, enlightenment; inspire you."*[22]

Oprah says a talk show doesn't have to do all these things all the time, but if you leave the show feeling better about yourself, your day, your life, she has done her job.

∽

Some of the topics covered on shows in the past several years include "Women Wrestling with Finances," "Loss of Sexual Desire in Women," "Heroic Acts," "Amazing El Niño Stories," "Nobody Knows I'm Homeless," "Conjoined Twins," "Little Girls Obsessed by Love," "Night Terrors" (sleep disorders), and "Incredible Friendship Stories."

∽

Oprah's decision to elevate the level of her television shows may have been spurred by the 1990 death of a young man who committed suicide not long after appearing on her show entitled "Bad-Influence Friends." The man's family claimed that he'd been hounded on the street after a show in which the studio audience berated him for living his life to party, being unfaithful to his wife, and other faults.

Nevertheless, Oprah has been able to measure the positive results of some shows. She helped nab a suspected murderer, when she invited John Walsh of *America's Most Wanted* to review the most difficult unsolved crimes on her show. John Hawkins was wanted by authorities, under suspicion of staging the death of his business partner to collect $2.5 million in insurance money. Hawkins and two partners allegedly murdered a drifter and tried to pass the body off as that of the business partner. A girlfriend in Holland turned Hawkins in after Oprah's show aired there.[23]

~

Oprah's ratings sometimes have slipped from their top slot in the increasingly crowded and competitive afternoon talk show field, presumably because of her insistence on taking a higher ground. Yet, Oprah sticks to her guns.

"I will continue to use The Oprah Winfrey Show *to discuss serious issues."*[24]

~

OPRAH'S WORST MISTAKES

PLEASING OTHERS ISN'T EVERYTHING

"You know what my biggest fault is? I don't have the courage to be disliked."[1]

~

"I was one of the children who was abused because I couldn't say no, because it was more important for me to please the abuser than to please myself. I didn't want the . . . boys to be mad at me."[2]

~

"Throughout my life I have done the most incredible things for men who treated me like s———. For my first boyfriend I remember going into the kitchen and making an omelet. If it was a little lopsided, I threw it out and started over, to make sure it was perfect."[3]

~

Over the years Oprah has learned that she can't please everyone all the time. She's had to quit posing for pictures with fans after the show because it takes too much time and energy. She no longer hugs fans she meets in public, because the toll is too heavy on her sense of personal privacy.[4]

~

It was difficult for Oprah to change her mind, after signing a contract to publish her life story. After a splashy party at the 1993 American Booksellers Association meeting in Miami announcing her autobiography, Oprah shocked the publishing world and disappointed her publisher, Alfred A. Knopf, by withdrawing the book. She'd already written it with the help of Joan Barthel and the publisher had arranged a staggering first printing of 1 million copies.

There were rumors that Oprah withdrew the book because Stedman Graham objected to personal material and graphic sexual passages. The *New York Daily News* said Stedman laid down the law to Winfrey: "Publish, and our engagement perishes."[5] Oprah denies that was the reason.

Winfrey said while the book did a good job of recounting the events of her life, she had hoped for more:

> *"I wanted to offer some insight, some clarity and some wisdom that might benefit other people."*

~

She felt that the time wasn't yet right for an autobiography. Right now, Oprah said:

"I'm in the heart of a learning curve."[6]

~

According to some reports, Oprah received a $4 million advance from Knopf, although other sources say that she never actually signed a contract with the publisher. Whatever the case, in lieu of her own book, Oprah arranged for Knopf to publish *In the Kitchen with Rosie: Oprah's Favorite Recipes*, Bob Greene's exercise book *Making the Connection*, and other Oprah-related projects. The 1994 cookbook by Oprah's chef, Rosie Daley, has sold more than 6 million copies so far. Greene's book sold more than 2 million. Knopf said it would wait for Oprah's memoir and publish it whenever she was ready.[7]

~

Although her autobiography still is not published, Oprah says that writing it was worth 10 years of therapy:

> *"As I peeled away the layers of my life, I realized that all my craziness, all my pain and difficulties, stemmed from me not valuing myself. And what I now know is that every single bit of pain I have experienced in my life was a result of me worrying about what another person was going to think of me."*[8]

~

Oprah sometimes has been at odds with black community leaders. In college, she felt out of place because the civil rights movement was in full force, and she didn't want or need to be militant. The movie *The Color Purple* was criticized because of its negative portrayal of black men, and when *The Women of Brewster Place* went into production, the National Association for the Advancement of Colored People asked to review the script in advance. She was insulted by the request:

> *"I am just as concerned about the images of black men as anybody, but there are black men who abuse their families, and there are white men who do it, too, and brown men. It's just a fact of life. I deal with it every day. So, I refuse to be controlled by other people's ideas and ideas of what I should do."*[9]

Oprah also has riled animal rights activists with her passion for fur coats. In 1990 she spent $1 million for five furs:

> *"I say minks were born to die."*[10]

Perhaps her love of furs has something to do with the frigid Chicago weather. She arrived in the windy city just before Christmas of 1984, and when she tried to walk to the corner store, the icy wind blew her down:

> *"This cold was awesome, it was serious cold. I thought I was delirious in the streets! Negroes weren't built for this kind of weather! We start praying for the motherland!"*[11]

～

To get an idea of all the people Oprah displeases, log on to the Internet. Pro-gun activists protest her shows promoting gun safety with children. One firearms activist compiled a list of companies that advertised on the shows so that their products could be boycotted. Gay men objected to the filming of the Harpo movie *The Wedding* in North Carolina because they say politicians there are antigay. Vegetarians protested Oprah's statement saying that she would eat only turkey after learning more about mad cow disease. "Please protest. Tell Oprah that turkeys bred for food production are miserable, sick and badly treated . . . Tell Oprah to promote the Turkey's Golden Rule: Don't Gobble Me!"[12]

～

Although she has stopped trying to please everyone, Oprah still tries to be nice. When invited by President Clinton to dine at the White House, she obliged a request to detour and visit the kitchen staff.

OTHERS SPEAK ABOUT OPRAH

THE FANS

Busloads of fans stop outside Oprah's highrise apartment building just to see where she lives. Many leave food and other gifts for her with the doorman. John Navarino, general manager KABC-TV, says that she has all kinds of fans.

"Oprah relates to the common denominator in all viewers."[1]

~

Geraldo Rivera says of Oprah, "Despite tremendous success, she still has the patina of 'I've suffered like you; therefore I understand you.'"[2]

~

Roger Ailes, president of the cable channel CNBC, sees it this way:

"With all the power and all the money, she could have become Leona Helmsley, but she didn't, and that's really the secret to Oprah."[3]

~

"I find all of Oprah's shows have something positive about them," said Lannie Smith, a 50-year-old paramedic from Miami, "something you can learn from. I have gone to a course in miracles, and I knew she's had [New Age self-help guru] Marianne Williamson on, which is how I learned about it. And that one thing changed my life."[4]

~

There are many Oprah Winfrey discussion groups, chat rooms, and so forth on the Internet, including the show's official Web site, www.Oprah.com.

Almost as ubiquitous as the official Web site has been the site called *Rachel's Ode to Oprah Winfrey*, produced by a third-year computer systems engineering student at the University of Guelph in Ontario, Canada. Rachel got a taste of how rich and famous people are treated and at last report was considering shutting down her Web site, for the following reasons.

1. Too many ungrateful Oprah fans who can't comprehend that ALL I KNOW IS ON MY WEBSITE!

2. Too many ungrateful Oprah fans who complain to me when I DO answer their e-mails with something like "Use the HELP page." They say I am not 'nice' enough in my response.

3. Lack of cooperation, comprehension, collaboration of this Web site's many frequent visitors. (I realize this doesn't apply to some/many of you.)

In case Rachel is still there, you can check out her Web site at www.virtual-space.com. But please, be nice.[5]

~

Despite Rachel's trauma, Oprah says fans make up 20-fold for anything she lacked in her childhood. She was crossing a street in New York when a woman approached her:

"I want to tell you how much I appreciate your evolution. I appreciate the fact that you are open enough to let us see it, because when I see that you can do it, I feel I can."

At that point, recalls Oprah, "I wanted to weep on the street 'cause I thought, 'You get it.' To me, that's better than any award, it's better than um, um, I don't know if it's better than a 13 rating, though."

Oprah flopped back on the couch, her legs in the air, in peals of laughter. "Yeah, I'll take the 13.2, yes I will."[6]

NOTE: Some fans have had to wait up to two years for tickets to the show. It may take even longer. After calling for several months at all hours of the workday, it seemed clear the ticket line is continually busy. Those who are getting tickets are unlikely to be obtaining them through the telephone number listed on the Oprah Winfrey Web site or printed on cards handed out by her staff.

~

According to Dr. Howard Garrell, a New York psycho-analyst, talk show viewers are happier, healthier, and better adjusted than nonviewers:

"They're better informed about health matters, complain less about loneliness and insecurity, feel more in control of their lives—and enjoy better relationships with their spouses and children."[7]

~

When Oprah was given the *Ladies' Home Journal* "One Smart Lady" award in 1995, she said:

"There are days when I've made the same mistake 14 times, and I say, 'Do I have any sense?' Now I have an award to prove that I do. So every time I'm in the mistake pit, I'm going to say, 'One day I was one smart lady—and I had 400 witnesses.'"[8]

THE CRITICS

Oprah doesn't have many critics, but they do exist. In 1988 Jeff Jarvis of *People's Weekly* suggested that Oprah's shows were trashy by simply listing his top-10 favorites:

1. Hairdresser Horror Stories
2. Housewife Prostitutes
3. Men Who Can't Be Intimate
4. Men Who Fight Over Women
5. Man-Stealing Relatives
6. Polygamy
7. Unforgivable Acts Between Couples
8. Sexy Dressing
9. Get Rich and Quit Work
10. Women Who Are Allergic to Their Husbands[9]

Barbara Grizzuti Harrison wrote a scathing article for *The New York Times Magazine* about *The Oprah Winfrey Show*:

"You'll forgive me, but it's white trailer trash. It debases language, it debases emotion. It provides everyone with glib psychological formulas. [These people] go around talking like a fortune cookie. And I think she is in very large part responsible for that."[10]

∼

Some of the criticism comes from revelations about the show—"the cathode confessional"—itself. It turned out that at least one guest, Tani Freiwald, a married woman who claimed to hate sex, was a fraud. She actually was an actress and former receptionist for a Chicago area sex therapist. Freiwald and an actor friend also made appearances on the Geraldo Rivera and Sally Jesse Raphael shows.

Oprah's executive producer said, "We take every precaution to ensure a person's credibility. We trusted the referral of Chicago psychologist Dr. Dean Dauw, who specializes in sex therapy."[11]

~

Occasionally guests on *The Oprah Winfrey Show* have accused Oprah and her staff of trapping them into situations that were humiliating or not factually accurate. A teenager who appeared on a show about girls who become pregnant on purpose said later that her pregnancy was not intentional, and when she went on the show, she was not aware that she would be placed in a confrontational situation with the audience.[12]

Misunderstandings do occur. In 1987, two years after the Challenger space shuttle exploded killing the seven members of its crew, Oprah invited the relatives of the crew to be on her show. Later, Jane Scobee, widow of Challenger commander Francis Scobee, and Marcia Jarvis, widow of Challenger scientist Gregory Jarvis, claimed they were told the session would concentrate on plans for the Challenger Center, a memorial space education center to be built in Washington, D.C.

Instead, Winfrey posed upsetting personal questions about the family's grief, bitterness, and whether they believed the crew members knew they were about to die.

"This was tough," said Scobee, "recalling the difficulty and problems associated with the loss. I generally don't respond to those questions. Our focus was to turn the tragedy into something positive for the country."[13]

Winfrey told reporters she didn't believe the Challenger families were misled:

> *"I don't feel that we exploited the families at all. If we had thought that the families weren't willing to talk about their emotions, we never would have done the show. We wouldn't have done a show just to talk about the Challenger Center."[14]*

~

Oprah deeply offended many Jewish people during a show on cults, in which she interviewed a woman who claimed that she suffered multiple personality disorder as a result of being forced into a satanic cult. The woman contended that she was of the Jewish faith and that, for generations, her family had sacrificed babies in religious ceremonies. Winfrey met with Jewish leaders after the show, then issued this statement:

"We recognize that *The Oprah Winfrey Show* of May 1 could have contributed to the perpetuation of historical misconceptions and canards about Jews, and we regret that any harm may have been done. We have and will continue to be sensitive to group and community sensibilities."[15]

~

Spy magazine once described Oprah this way:

"Capaciously built, black, and extremely noisy, Oprah Winfrey is an aberration among talk show doyennes, and her press materials bleat as much. She is awash in adjectival suds: earthy, spontaneous, genuine, brassy, down-home. 'The adorable token dumpling' is how one public relations executive describes her. A hyperkinetic amalgam of Mae West, Reverend Ike, Richard Simmons, and Hulk Hogan is more to the point."[16]

LOOKING AHEAD

STRETCHING THE LIMITS

Through good times and bad, Oprah continues to strive:

> *"My goal for myself is to reach the highest level of humanity that is possible to me. Then, when I'm done, when I quit the planet, I want to be able to say, 'Boy, I did that, didn't I? Yes, I did!' And I want to get up there and high-five with the angels. High-five with them and have them say, 'Yes, girl, you did it. You really did it!'"*[1]

As Oprah becomes increasingly involved in restructuring her show, making movies, and finding other challenging, worthy projects, she says:

> *"On my own I will just create, and if it works it works, and if it doesn't, I'll create something else. I don't have any limitations now on what I think I could do or be."*[2]

"I believe you're here to live your life with passion. Otherwise, you're just traveling through the world blindly—and there's no point to that."[3]

~

"Don't complain about what you don't have. Use what you've got. To do less than your best is a sin. Every single one of us has the power for greatness, because greatness is determined by service—to yourself and to others."[4]

~

"When I first started this, people used to say to me— usually relatives who wanted money—'Honey, don't you think that this gonna las' fo'ever, 'cause you not gonna be on top all the time.' Well, I know that—and I don't necessarily believe this is the top. But I don't want to get lazy either. I don't want to be lulled by the voices of the world telling me something is It, *and buy into that."*[5]

~

". . . I believe that you tend to create your own blessings. You have to prepare yourself so that when opportunity comes, you're ready."[6]

THE PROGRESS SO FAR

When the demands on her time, energy, and new money become overwhelming, Oprah falls back on the admonition of her friend and mentor Maya Angelou— you don't have to do it all:

"Baby, all you *have* to do is stay black and die ... The work is the thing, and what matters at the end of the day is, were you sweet, were you kind, did you get the work done?"[7]

~

With little doubt, Americans feel that Oprah is getting the work done. In a 1997 survey, Oprah ranked second only to Mother Teresa in a poll asking who was most likely to go to heaven. When it came to Mother Teresa, 79 percent of those queried said she would be welcome inside the Pearly Gates; Oprah got 66 percent approval. Only 47 percent thought evangelist and founder of the Christian Coalition Pat Robertson would please St. Peter. More than 87 percent of those polled believe they themselves are likely to go to heaven.[8]

~

Oprah's lifetime theme has been transformation and growth—she's constantly seeking, questioning, changing, looking for her place and her power. On the wall of her Chicago apartment hangs the words of Glinda, the good witch in *The Wizard of Oz*:

"You don't need to be helped any longer. You've always had the power."[9]

~

Oprah once outlined the 10 commandments that guide her success:

1. Don't live your life to please others.

2. Don't depend on forces outside of yourself to get ahead.

3. Seek harmony and compassion in your business and personal life.

4. Get rid of the back-stabbers—surround yourself only with people who will lift you higher.

5. Be nice.

6. Rid yourself of your addictions—whether they be food, alcohol, drugs, or behavior habits.

7. Surround yourself with people who are as smart or smarter than yourself.

8. If money is your motivation, forget it.

9. Never hand over your power to someone else.

10. Be persistent in pursuing your dreams.[10]

~

When things were the darkest, belief in herself has helped Oprah go forward:

"I always knew I was going to do well in life. I always believed that whatever I wanted for myself I could get."[11]

~

"I was like a hit album waiting to be released. I knew my day would come."[12]

When Stedman Graham's daughter, Wendy, graduated from Wellesley College in 1997, Oprah delivered the commencement address. She told the graduates that she'd learned five important lessons that made her life better:

1. Life is a journey. Every day experiences will teach you who you really are.

2. When people show you who they are, believe them the first time. This is especially helpful with men. Don't force them to beat you over the head with the message.

3. Turn your wounds into wisdom. Everyone makes mistakes. They are just God's way of telling you you're moving in the wrong direction.

4. Be grateful. Keep a daily journal of the things you are thankful for. It will keep you focused on the abundance in your life.

5. Create the highest, grandest vision possible for your life because you become what you believe.[13]

Oprah once said:

"People have told me their lives have changed because of me. I take away from this the sense that I'm on the right track."[14]

Overall:

> *"The life I lead is good. People ask me what temperature I would like to have my tea . . . all things are possible."*[15]

AS LIFE GOES ON

As Oprah Winfrey moves into middle age, birthdays became an opportunity for growth and happiness:

> *"Whoopi Goldberg told me, when we were shooting* The Color Purple *that it—and I meant It with a capital I—doesn't even start to happen until you're 36. I took her at her word. And so, for me, this is the most exciting birthday I've ever had."*[16]

When she decided not to publish her memoirs, she explained:

> *"I feel there are important discoveries yet to be made."*[17]

> *"In your 20s and 30s you are always struggling to be open to what other people see as their vision for you. But you reach the point where you're not willing to accept the bull that you're used to."*[18]

Oprah has a vision of what she will be like as a senior citizen:

"Sure, Grandma whipped me, she sure did. But she taught me about life, and I loved her so. I'll look like her when I'm old. I'll be one of those spiritual ladies rockin' and shoutin' in the church. Yes, ma'am, you'll find me in the amen corner."[19]

WHAT'S AHEAD FOR OPRAH?

Oprah has achieved so much in her life it's easy to forget that she has many years ahead to make new and ever-expanding dreams come true.

In 1987 she predicted she would do the show only for five years more.

"These things have their own life. You determine for yourself what you want . . . In five years, I'll have done what I want in this format."[20]

～

That didn't happen, of course. She continued with the show, developing and expanding its reach and content. In a 1995 America Online interview, fans again tried to pin Oprah down by asking what she saw herself doing 10 years from now:

"That's a tough question for me. It shouldn't be, but it is. I live in the moment, for it's hard for me to see next week. I won't be doing this show 10 years from now. If I am, come drag my butt off! Thank you."[21]

～

Although she sometimes gets very tired, Oprah keeps going because she believes her show has a positive impact on society. When she is tired, she summons up the lines from one of her favorite spirituals:

"I'll run on, see what the end will be. I believe I will work on, see what the end will be."[22]

~

"When I look at the future it's so bright I burn my eyes."[23]

TIMELINE

1954 *January 29*: Oprah Winfrey was born in Kosciusko, Mississippi, the illegitimate child of Vernita Lee and Vernon Winfrey. That same year the U.S. Supreme Court, in *Brown v. Board of Education*, ruled that racial segregation in public schools is a violation of the 14th amendment of the Constitution.

1960 Oprah left Mississippi for Milwaukee to live with her mother and stepsister and later, her stepbrother. She excelled at school but ran wild at home.

1968 Her mother tried to place her in a juvenile hall but Oprah was turned away for lack of beds.

Fourteen-year-old Oprah gave birth to a premature boy, who died soon after birth.

Her father Vernon and his wife, Zelma, took Oprah into their Nashville home. In this new atmosphere Oprah became an honor student and was popular at school.

1970 WVOL Radio hired Oprah "Gail" Winfrey to read news on the air. She was paid $100 per week, an excellent salary for a 16-year-old.

1971 Oprah graduated from East Nashville High School and was voted "Most Popular." She won a four-year scholarship to Tennessee State University based on her speaking abilities.

Oprah was crowned Miss Black Tennessee.

1973 At 19, Oprah became the first African American woman ever to anchor the news at Nashville's WTVF-TV.

1976 WJZ-TV, Baltimore hired Oprah to host the 6 o'clock news.

Oprah met her lifetime pal, Gayle King, a production assistant at WJZ-TV.

1977 *April 1*: Oprah was demoted from news anchor to morning talk show host.

Oprah became cohost of *People Are Talking* on WJZ-TV, a job that lasted until 1983.

1984 Oprah Winfrey moved to Illinois to host *A.M. Chicago*.

1985 *The Oprah Winfrey Show* replaced *A.M. Chicago*; later in the year the show became nationally syndicated.

The Color Purple was released and Oprah was nominated for an Oscar for her performance as Sophia.

1986 The movie *Native Son* was released. In it Oprah plays a mother who begged for her son's life after he accidentally killed a young woman.

1987 Oprah won her first Emmy as outstanding talk/service show host, and *The Oprah Winfrey Show* is named best show.

February 9: Oprah aired what is considered by some critics to be her best show: It was from Forsyth County, Georgia, where no blacks had been allowed to live since 1912.

Tennessee State University granted Oprah a diploma, after refusing to waive her senior project in lieu of work experience. She got her degree in speech and drama, then delivered the commencement address.

Oprah played herself in the Danny DeVito movie, *Throw Momma from the Train*.

1988 Winfrey was named Broadcaster of the Year by the International Television and Radio Society. The youngest-ever recipient of that award, Winfrey joined the ranks of Walter Cronkite, David Brinkley, Barbara Walters, and Ted Koppel.

Winfrey obtained ownership and control of her show from Chicago's ABC-TV station, WLS. She began producing the show in the fall of 1988.

The National Conference of Christians and Jews gave Oprah their Humanitarian Award.

Oprah bought her Chicago studio facility and her farm in Indiana.

Billy Rizzo, Oprah's longtime assistant, died of AIDS.

Oprah was a guest star on *Pee-Wee Herman's Playhouse: Christmas Special*.

1989 Oprah starred as Mattie Michael in the movie *The Women of Brewster Place*.

The restaurant in which Oprah was an investor—The Eccentric—opened in Chicago.

Oprah's half brother Jeffrey Lee died of AIDS.

Using the Optifast liquid diet, Oprah reduced her weight to 142 pounds, allowing her to fit into a size 10 dress. She celebrated by dragging a 67-pound slab of animal fat onto her show. She soon regained the pounds she lost.

1990 *Brewster Place*, a weekly television show that Oprah produced and starred in, closed after just 10 weeks.

Oprah played herself in the movie *Listen Up: The Lives of Quincy Jones.*

On a show in which she interviewed child sexual abuse victim Truddi Chase, Oprah revealed that she too had been molested as a child.

Oprah regains 70 pounds.

1991 Oprah initiated the National Child Protection Act and testified before Congress.

Oprah hired California spa chef Rosie Daley to supervise a new and healthier diet.

1992 Stedman Graham and Oprah Winfrey became engaged and, to her later regret, Oprah announced the proposal on national television.

When Oprah won Best Talk Show Host at the Daytime Emmy Awards, she was miserable. She weighed 237 pounds, her highest weight ever.

Oprah found Colorado trainer Bob Greene to supervise her exercise program.

1993 With Oprah looking on, President Bill Clinton signed the National Child Protection Act.

Oprah produced and starred in the made-for-TV movie, *There Are No Children Here.*

Oprah took up running and began to lose the nearly 80 pounds she gained following her liquid diet.

Publishing company Alfred E. Knopf signed Winfrey for an alleged $4 million contract for her biography. In the summer of 1993, Winfrey withdrew the finished book and it was never published.

Oprah lost 72 pounds. Although her weight battle continues, she kept most of this weight off.

1994 Oprah won Best Talk Show and Best Talk Show Host at the 21st Annual Daytime Emmy Awards.

Debra DiMaio and two other staff members left *The Oprah Winfrey Show*, and Oprah is criticized for not making personnel changes sooner.

In the Kitchen with Rosie: Oprah's Favorite Recipes, was published by Knopf, seen as a palliative for the withdrawal of Oprah's own book the year before.

1995 *January 13*: Oprah Winfrey admitted on a broadcast television show that 20 years earlier she had used the illegal drug cocaine.

Oprah became the first woman to head the Forbes Top 40 Entertainers list, a ranking of entertainers by their income. She also was the only entertainer and the only black on Forbes' list of 400 richest Americans.

Winfrey won an Emmy for Best Talk Show and Best Host for the second year in a row.

The Walt Disney Co. contracted with Oprah to produce and star in several motion pictures over the next five years. The terms of the deal were not disclosed.

"Oprah Online" debuted on America Online in partnership with ABC.

Indecent exposure charges were dropped against Oprah's father, Vernon Winfrey.

1996 Oprah received the most prestigious award in broadcasting, the George Foster Peabody's Individual Achievement Award.

April 16: *The Oprah Winfrey Show* dealt with mad cow disease in the United States. Winfrey was subsequently sued under a "veggie libel" law in Texas that prohibits false product disparagement.

April 23: Dr. Gary Weber of the National Cattlemen's Beef Association and cattle rancher Connie

Greig appeared on Oprah's show to refute implications of an earlier show that eating beef could expose Americans to a deadly brain disease.

September 16: Oprah announced the start of her successful on-air reading club.

1997 *Before Women Had Wings*, starring Oprah Winfrey and produced by her, aired on ABC television. The show helped make ABC number 1 in the Nielsen ratings for the week.

Bob Greene and Oprah Winfrey's video, *Oprah: Make the Connection*, was released.

The Wedding, a four-hour miniseries directed by Charles Burnett and starring Halle Berry, was produced and released under the banner Oprah Winfrey Presents.

Oprah announced the formation of Oprah's Angel Network, a national effort to encourage viewers to make charitable contributions and to do volunteer work.

Oprah delivered the commencement address to the Wellesley College Class of 1997.

1998 *February 26*: Oprah prevailed in defending herself in the food disparagement lawsuit brought by Texas cattlemen.

Oprah received a Lifetime Achievement Award from the Daytime Emmy Awards, plus an award for top talk show host.

Harpo Entertainment had the movie version of the Toni Morrison novel, *Beloved*, in production.

ENDNOTES

Preface

1. "The Year's Most Admired," *People Online Daily*, January 1–2, 1998.
2. "Post-Seinfeld," *Los Angeles Times*, Friday, May 15, 1998, p. F1.
3. Elise O'Shaughnessy, "The New Establishment," *Vanity Fair*, October 1994, p. 209.
4. Walter Scott, "Personality Parade," *Parade*, May 3, 1998, p. 4.
5. "Oprah Winfrey Inducted into TV Hall of Fame," *Jet*, October 17, 1994, p. 8.
6. "Oprah Winfrey to Receive the Horatio Alger Award," *Jet*, February 1, 1993, p. 52.
7. "And That's the Way It Isn't," *People*, August 29, 1994, p. 35.
8. Christopher Little, "Oprah Winfrey," *People's Weekly*, December 20, 1987, p. 74.
9. George Mair, *Oprah Winfrey: The Real Story* (Secaucus, N. J.: Birch Lane Press, 1994), p. 275.

A Woman of Influence

1. "Oprah Winfrey: Talk-Show Host," *Time*, June 17, 1996, p. 65.
2. Maarten Huygen, "The Invasion of the American Way," *World Press Review*, November 1992, p. 28.
3. John Culhane, "Oprah Winfrey: How Truth Changed Her Life," *Reader's Digest*, February 1989, p. 102.
4. "Oprah Named Favorite Air Flight Seatmate in Poll," *Jet*, August 30, 1993, p. 35.
5. Mark Steyn, "Comic Oprah: American's Talker-in-Chief Is the Perfect Embodiment of the Virtual Culture of the Nineties," *National Review*, March 23, 1998, p. 30.
6. "Oprah Winfrey Will Continue to Host and Produce *The Oprah Winfrey Show* into the Next Century," New York, Entertainment Wire, September 15, 1997.

7. George Mair, *Oprah Winfrey: The Real Story* (Secaucus, N. J.: Birch Lane Press, 1994), p. 267.

8. "Queen Oprah," *The Wall Street Journal*, September 17, 1977, p. A22.

9. Steyn, "Comic Oprah," p. 30.

Oprah's Roots

1. Barbara Grizzuti Harrison, "The Importance of Being Oprah," *The New York Times Magazine*, June 11, 1989, p. 30.

2. Elaine Warren, "There's Oprah, Jackee, Robin Givens—and a Break Men May Not Deserve," *TV Guide*, March 18, 1989, p. 4.

3. Rosie Daley, *In the Kitchen with Rosie* (New York: Alfred A. Knopf, 1996), p. xi.

4. Norman King, *Everybody Loves Oprah: Her Remarkable Life Story* (New York: Quill, William Morrow, 1987), p. 35.

5. Robert Waldron, *Oprah!* (New York: St. Martin's Press, 1987), p. 19.

6. Andre Walker, *Andre Talks Hair* (New York: Simon & Schuster, 1997), p. 11.

7. Alan Richman, "Oprah," *People Weekly*, January 12, 1987, p. 50.

8. Ibid.

9. Ibid.

10. Kinny Littlefield, "Oprah Still Enjoying Her Power," *St. Louis Post-Dispatch*, May 28, 1997, p. 3E.

11. Audrey Edwards, "Stealing the Show," *Essence*, October 1986, p. 52.

12. Ann Saidman, *Oprah Winfrey: Media Success Story* (Minneapolis: Lerner Publications, 1990), p. 42.

13. Richard C. Firstman, "Oprah Power," *Newsday*, November 1, 1989, p. 4.

14. Judy Markey, "Opinionated Oprah," *Woman's Day*, October 4, 1988, p. 71.

15. Waldron, *Oprah!*, pp. 42–43.

16. Susan Taylor, "An Intimate Talk with Oprah," *Essence*, August 1987, p. 58.

17. Al Cohn, ed., "Premature Child Died," *Newsday*, May 2, 1990, p. 8.

18. Laura B. Randolph, "Oprah Opens Up About Her Weight, Her Wedding and Why She Withheld the Book," *Ebony*, October 1993, p. 131.

19. Ibid.

20. Richman, "Oprah."

21. Nellie Bly, *Oprah! Up Close and Down Home* (New York: Zebra Books, 1993), p. 87.

22. Ibid.

23. Lisa DePaulo, "Oprah's Private Life: The Inside Story," *TV Guide*, June 3, 1989, p. 2.

24. "The Best Christmas I Ever Had," *Ebony*, December 1991, p. 54.

25. Robert Waldron, *Oprah!*, p. 15.

26. Ibid., p. 43.

27. Robert Sanders, "TV Host Oprah Winfrey," *People Weekly*, December 16, 1985, p. 42.

28. Norman King, "Oprah," *Good Housekeeping*, August 1987, p. 108.

29. Waldron, *Oprah!*, pp. 42–43.

30. Maureen Olsen, "Oprah Winfrey," miavx1.muohio.edu/~edpcwis/ Olsen_Oprah.html.

31. The Hall of Business, Interview, February 21, 1991, www.achievement.org.

32. Jill Brooke Coiner, "Oprah Sets the Record Straight," *McCall's*, November 1993, p. 148.

33. Oprah Winfrey, "Lady with a Calling," *Time*, August 8, 1988, p. 62.

34. Susan Letwin, "Oprah Opens Up," *TV Guide*, May 5, 1990, p. 6.

35. "Honors Her Father," *Jet*, August 31, 1987, p. 19.

36. "Oprah Winfrey Responds to Allegations That Her Father Harassed College Student," *Jet*, February 20, 1995, p. 18.

37. "Greedy Lawyer Jailed for Putting Squeeze on Oprah's Dad," 1996, www.tvtalkshows.com.

You Are Responsible for Your Life

1. Marcia Ann Gillespie, "Winfrey Takes All," *Ms.*, November 1988, p. 54.

2. "Oprah Winfrey Gives Another Million to Morehouse College: Graduates Call Her 'An Angel,' " *Jet*, December 8, 1997, p. 22.

3. "Oprah Winfrey Gives Gift of $1 Million to Morehouse to Help Educate Black Men," *Jet*, June 5, 1989, p. 4.

4. Stedman Graham, *You Can Make It Happen Every Day* (New York: Simon & Schuster, 1998), p. 136.

5. Oprah Winfrey, Interview, America Online, October 3, 1995.

6. Nellie Bly, *Oprah! Up Close and Down Home* (New York: Zebra Books, 1993), p. 24.

7. Bill Adler, *The Uncommon Wisdom of Oprah Winfrey* (Secaucus, N. J.: Birch Lane Press, 1997), p. 52.

8. "Oprah Donates $100,000 to Harold Washington Library," *Jet*, October 7, 1991, p. 18.

9. Alan Ebert, "Oprah Winfrey Talks Openly about Oprah," *Good Housekeeping*, September 1991, p. 62.

10. Matthew Flamm, "Book 'em, Oprah," *Entertainment Weekly*, October 25, 1998.

11. Marilyn Johnson and Dana Fineman, "Oprah Winfrey: A Life in Books," *Life*, September 1997, p. 9.

12. Ibid.

13. "Paradise Found," *Time*, January 19, 1998.

14. Michael Shain, "Oprah's Books Are Fodder for Her TV Empire," *New York Post*, 1998, www.nypostonline.com.

15. Maureen Olsen, "Oprah Winfrey," miavx1.muohio.edu/~educwis/ Olsen_Oprah.html.

16. "Oprah's Current Selection," Barnes & Noble.com, Web site.

17. "Oprah Winfrey," *Entertainment Weekly*, December 27, 1996, p. 36.

18. "Books for Kids Recommended on the June 18 Oprah Show," www.alt.bookstore.com.

19. Michael Shain, "Oprah's Books Are Fodder for Her TV Empire," *New York Post*, 1998, www.nypostonline.com.

20. Pam Anderson Bared, "Oprah vs. Rodman," *People Online Daily*, April 29, 1997.

21. Bitch of the Week Web site, www.bitch.com.

22. Pamela Noel, "Lights! Camera! Oprah!" *Ebony*, April 1986, p. 105.

23. Sara Mosle, "Grand New Oprah," *Savvy*, August 1988, p. 20.

24. Oprah Winfrey, "TV's Super Women," *Ladies' Home Journal*, March 1988, p. 168.

25. Daytime Emmy Awards, NBC Television, May 15, 1998.

26. Bly, *Oprah!*, p. 64.

27. Pamela Jones, "Fine Tuning!" *Essence*, July 1985, p. 46.

28. "No Guts, No Glory: Oprah as Survivor," *McCall's*, August 1995, p. 76.

29. Robert La Franco, "Piranha Is Good," *Forbes 400*, October 16, 1995, p. 68.

30. Kathleen Fury, "Oprah! Why She's Got America Talking," *TV Guide*, March 5, 1988, p. 27.

31. "Oprah Winfrey Tells Why Blacks Who Bash Blacks Tick Her Off," *Jet*, September 17, 1990, p. 62.

32. "Oprah Winfrey," *People Weekly*, December 27, 1993.

33. Marjorie Rosen, "Oprah Overcomes," *People Weekly*, January 10, 1994, p. 42.

34. Oprah Winfrey, Speech, 44th National Convention, National Council of Negro Women, Washington, D.C., December 4, 1989.

35. Julia Cameron, "Simply Oprah," *Cosmopolitan*, February 1989, p. 215.

36. "Oprah Winfrey Tells Why"

37. Alan Richman, "Oprah," *People Weekly*, January 12, 1987, p. 56.

38. R. C. Smith, "She Once Trashed Her Apartment to Make a Point," *TV Guide*, August 30, 1986, p. 31.

39. "Lady with a Calling: Oprah Winfrey," www.Time100.com.

40. "Woods Stars on Oprah, Says He's 'Cablinasian,'"Associated Press, Chicago, April 23, 1997.

41. Robert Waldron, *Oprah!* (New York: St. Martin's Press, 1987), p. 84.

Finding Her Niche

1. George Mair, *Oprah Winfrey: The Real Story* (Secaucus, N.J.: Birch Lane Press, 1994), p. 44.

2. Robert Waldron, *Oprah!* (New York: St. Martin's Press, 1987), p. 68.

3. "Oprah Winfrey," *Vanity Fair*, October 1994.

4. Mair, *Oprah Winfrey*, p. 31.

5. Chris Anderson, "Meet Oprah Winfrey," *Good Housekeeping*, August 1986, p. 32.

6. Pamela Johnson, "Fine Tuning!" *Essence*, July 1985, p. 46.

7. Ibid.

8. Pamela Noel, "Lights! Camera! Oprah!" *Essence*, April 1985, p. 105.

9. Barbara Laker, "Cattle Ranchers Should've Know: Oprah Just Doesn't Lose," *San Diego Union Tribune*, March 6, 1998, p. E-3.

10. Larry Martin, "The Daily Celebrity News," *People Online Daily*, March 7–8, 1998.

11. "Golden Bloopers," www.ewonline.com, December 25, 1997.

12. Stephen Braun, "How Oprah Reinvented Her Talk Show and Became America's No. 1 Tastemaker," *Los Angeles Times*, March 9, 1997, p. 9.

13. Mair, *Oprah Winfrey*, p. 47.

14. "Oprah Winfrey's Success Story," *Ladies' Home Journal*, March, 1987, p. 64.

15. Drew Fetherson, "Oprah Winfrey Has Arrived," *Newsday*, September 8, 1986, C1.

16. Deborah Tannen, "Oprah Winfrey," *Time100*, www.Time100.com.

17. "Oprah Winfrey, 32, the Exception That Proves the Rule in Talk Show Hosts," *People Weekly*, August 25, 1986, p. 69.

18. "Oprah Winfrey: A Good Neighbor to Invite for a Chat," *Newsday*, September 10, 1986, p. C1.

19. Lyn Tornabene, "Here's Oprah," *Woman's Day*, October 1, 1986, p. 50.

20. Steven Braun, "How Oprah Reinvented Her Talk Show and Became America's No. 1 Tastemaker," *Los Angeles Times*, March 9, 1997, C1.

21. "Oprah Winfrey," *Entertainment Weekly*, December 27, 1996, p. 36.

22. Mair, *Oprah Winfrey*, p. 77.

23. Jennifer Hollettt, "Oprah Winfrey: Talk Show Host and Friend," Oprah.html@cug.concordia.ca.

24. Gretchen Reynolds, "Oprah Unbound," *Chicago*, November 1993, p. 86.

25. "Oprah Throws a Party," *Ebony*, June 1993, p. 120.

26. Diane Bell, "A Research Project that Bombed," *San Diego Union Tribune*, April 28, 1998, p. B-2.

27. Lawrence Van Gelder, "Footlights," *The New York Times*, April 8, 1998.

28. Richard Shay, "Oprah Throws a Party," *Ebony*, June 1993, p. 121.

29. Maya Angelou, "Oprah Winfrey," *Ms.*, January/February 1989, p. 88.

30. J. Randy Taraborrelli, "The Change That Has Made Oprah So Happy," *Redbook*, May 1997, p. 94.

31. Jeff B. Copeland, "Rosie Beats Oprah in L.A.," *E! Online*, February 28, 1997.

32. Kinny Littlefield, "Oprah Still Enjoying Her Power," *St. Louis Post-Dispatch*, May 28, 1997, p. 3E.

33. David Bauder, "Oprah, Rosie Tie at Daytime Emmys," Associated Press, May 18, 1998.

34. "Oprah: Yep, She's Straight," *People Online Daily*, June 5, 1997.

35. Claire Bickley, "Oprah Audience Generally Unsympathetic to Ellen," *Toronto Sun*, May 1, 1997.

36. "He Sure Looks Like Oprah," *People*, April 29, 1991, p. 120.

37. Associated Press, "He Wins Ladies' Oprah Search," *Newsday*, April 13, 1991, p. 2.

38. "He Sure Looks Like Oprah."

39. Verne Gay, "Fall Preview/Local Stations," *Newsday*, September 7, 1997, p. 13.

40. Jim Calio, "If You Knew Oprah Like I Know Oprah," *Redbook*, February 1998, p. 112.

41. "Seven Stars Say—What Makes a Good Friend," *Redbook*, October 1989, p. 22.

42. Lisa DePaulo, "Oprah's Private Life: The Inside Story," *TV Guide*, June 3, 1989, p. 3.

43. "Gayle King Makes Talk Show History with Oprah and Stedman," *Jet*, October 20, 1997, p. 54.

44. Gail Pennington, "Oprah's Buddy Has Own Show," *St. Louis Post-Dispatch*, August 26, 1997, p. 3D.

45. Audrey Edwards, "Girl Talk," *Ladies' Home Journal*, October 1997, p. 136.

46. "Syndicated TV Host, Gayle King," *People Online Chat*, February 25, 1998.

47. Susan King, "Functional TV," *Los Angeles Times*, September 7, 1997, TV Times, p. 5.

48. Kenneth Best, "Q&A: Gayle King: on Television, for News and Talk, Too," *The New York Times*, March 29, 1998.

49. Ibid.

50. Colin Bessonette, "Q&A on the News," *Atlanta Journal and Constitution*, September 22, 1997, p. A02.

51. Heike Donyavi, "Letters, Faxes & E-mail," *Atlanta Journal and Constitution*, September 10, 1997, p. A12.

52. Pennington, "Oprah's Buddy Has Own Show," *St. Louis Post-Dispatch*, August 26, 1997, p. 3D.

53. "Gayle King Makes Talk Show History."

54. Edwards, "Girl Talk."

55. Best, "Q&A."

56. Marilyn Milloy, "Oprah Gets an Earful in Georgia," *Newsday*, February 10, 1987, p. 3.

57. Noel, "Lights! Camera! Oprah!" p. 102.

58. "Oprah Winfrey," *Entertainment Weekly*, December 27, 1996, p. 36.

59. Ibid.

60. Savannah J. Peeples, "Hanson Makes a Splash on Oprah," *Globe-News*, February 16, 1998.

61. Ibid.

62. Norman King, *Everybody Loves Oprah* (New York: William Morrow and Company, 1987), p. 123.

63. Ibid.

64. Noel, "Lights! Camera! Oprah!" p. 100.

65. George Mair, *Oprah Winfrey: The Real Story* (Secaucus, N. J.: Birch Lane Press, 1994), p. 78.

66. Debra Dickerson, "A Woman's Woman," *U.S. News & World Report*, September 29, 1997, p. 10.

67. Oprah, Professional History, ccwf.utexas.edu~kcapps/Oprah6.html.

68. *The Oprah Winfrey Show*, www.Peopleonline.com.

69. "Oprah Winfrey's Harpo Studio Signs Deal with ABC Television to Produce Six Made-For-TV Movies, *Jet*, June 12, 1995.

70. Susan Letwin, "Oprah Opens Up," *TV Guide*, May 5, 1990, p. 5.

71. Michel Marriott, "Frank Racial Dialogue Thrives on the Web," *The New York Times*, March 8, 1998.

72. Christopher John Farley, "Oprah Springs Eternal," *Time*, August 30, 1993, p. 15.

73. David Zurawik, "Oprah Enlarges Her Empire," November 1, 1997, www.SunspotTV.com.

74. Ibid.

75. Kathleen Fury, "Oprah! Why She's Got America Talking," *TV Guide*, March 5, 1988, p. 27.

Oprah the Chief Executive Officer

1. Paul Noglows, "Oprah: The Year of Living Dangerously," *Working Woman*, May 1994, p. 52.

2. Robert La Franco and Josh McHugh, "Piranha Is Good," *Forbes*, October 15, 1995, p. 66.

3. David Carter, "Cutting Out the Middleman," *Forbes*, October 1, 1990, p. 166.

4. Robert La Franco, "Piranha Is Good," *Forbes 400*, October 16, 1995, p. 68.

5. Fred Goodman, "Madonna and Oprah," *Working Woman*, December, 1991, p. 53.

6. Noglows, "Oprah."

7. John Dempsey, "Winfrey Will Produce, Own Her Show and Develop Others," *Variety*, August 10, 1988, p. 36.

8. Oprah Winfrey Show Web Site, Winter 1998.

9. Joe Dziemianowicz and Ziba Kasher, "The Oprah You Don't Know," *McCall's*, August 1995, p. 73.

10. "King World Productions Inc.," *Hoover's Company Capsules* (Austin, TX: Hoover's Inc., 1998).

11. George Mair, *Oprah Winfrey: The Real Story* (Secaucus, N. J.: Birch Lane Press, 1994), p.106.

12. Ibid, p. 113.

13. Martin Peers, "Update: Oprah Speculation Dents King World Stock," *Daily Variety*, September 3, 1997, p. 1.

14. Goodman, "Madonna and Oprah."

15. Granite Broadcasting Corporation Web site, www.granite.com.

16. "Oprah Winfrey, Media Magnate," *Esquire*, December 1989, p. 114.

17. Goodman, "Madonna and Oprah."

18. Gretchen Reynolds, "A Year to Remember: Oprah Grows Up," *TV Guide*, January 7, 1995, p. 15.

19. Gretchen Reynolds, "The Oprah Myth," *TV Guide*, July 23, 1994, p. 11.

20. Jackie Rogers, "Understanding Oprah," *Redbook*, September 1993, p. 134.

21. Cosby's $84 Million Makes Him Richest Entertainer," *Jet*, September 28, 1987, p. 52.

22. Goodman, "Madonna and Oprah."

23. Ibid.

24. Reynolds, "A Year to Remember."

25. Mair, *Oprah Winfrey*, p. 341.

26. Leslie Rubenstein, "Oprah! Thriving on Faith," *McCall's*, August 1987, p. 140.

27. Reynolds, "The Oprah Myth," p. 9.

28. Dan Santow, "Christmas at Oprah's," *Redbook*, December 1994, p. 82.

29. Katharine Kest, "What Oprah Really Wants," *Redbook*, August 1995, p 77.

30. Robert Feder, "Ex-Publicist, Oprah Quietly Settle Law Suit," *Chicago Sun-Times*, May 21, 1996.

31. Dana Kennedy, "A New Soap Oprah," *Entertainment Weekly*, November 11, 1994, p. 10.

32. Reynolds, "The Oprah Myth," p. 14.

33. "Oprah Winfrey's Success Story," *Ladies' Home Journal*, March 1987, p. 64.

34. Lyn Tornabene, "Here's Oprah," *Woman's Day*, October 1986, p. 52.

35. Laura Fording, "Pop-Up Oprah," *Newsweek*, November 13, 1997.

36. Richard Zoglin, "Lady with a Calling," *Time*, August 8, 1988, p. 62.

37. Mair, *Oprah Winfrey*, p. 242.

38. Linden Gross, "Oprah Winfrey, Wonder Woman," *Ladies' Home Journal*, December 1988, p. 40.

39. Goodman, "Madonna and Oprah," p. 52.

40. Melina Gerosa, "Oprah: Fit for Life," *Ladies' Home Journal*, February 1996, p. 108.

41. Joanna Powell, "I Was Trying to Fill Something Deeper," *Good Housekeeping*, October 1996, p. 80.

42. Pearl Cleage, "Walking in the Light," *Essence*, June 1991, p. 48.

43. Eric Sherman, "Oprah's Wonder Year," *Ladies' Home Journal*, May 1990, p. 222.

On Living with Fame and Fortune

1. Judy Markey, "Brassy, Sassy Oprah Winfrey," *Cosmopolitan*, September 1986, p. 96.

2. Chris Anderson, "Meet Oprah Winfrey," *Good Housekeeping*, August 1986, p. 32.

3. Kim Cunningham, "Behind Closed Doors," *People Weekly*, April 29, 1996.

4. Oprah Winfrey, "TV's Super Women," *Ladies' Home Journal*, March 1988, p. 168.

5. Lyle Slack, "Alien Brainchild Lands in Supermarket, Libels Oprah, Dies," *Saturday Night*, November 1992, p. 18.

6. "Oprah Winfrey and Beau Win Defamation Suit Against Tabloid by Default," *Jet*, May 18, 1992, p. 60.

7. Stedman Graham, *You Can Make It Happen* (New York: Simon & Schuster, 1997), p. 44.

8. David Friedman, "Power, For a Price," *Newsday*, January 17, 1989, p. 9.

9. Ibid.

10. *The Ed Gordon Show*, May 30, 1995.

11. Ibid.

12. Louise Lague, "The White Tie House: Celebs Fete Japan's Emperor and Empress at the Clintons' First State Dinner," *People Weekly*, June 27, 1994, p. 38.

13. Oprah Winfrey, Graduation Address, Wesleyan University, Middletown, Connecticut, May 1998.

14. "Chat with Oprah," America Online, October 3, 1995.

15. Sara Mosle, "Grand New Oprah," *Savvy*, August 1988, p. 20.

16. Luchina Fisher, Steve Dale, and Sabrina McFarland, "In Full Stride," *People Weekly*, September 12, 1994, p. 84.

17. J. Randy Taraborrelli, "The Change That Has Made Oprah So Happy," *Redbook*, May 1997, p. 94.

18. Susan Taylor, "An Intimate Talk with Oprah," *Essence*, August 1987, p. 57.

19. Alan Ebert, "Oprah Winfrey Talks Openly About Oprah," *Good Housekeeping*, September 1991, p. 62.

20. "Six Ways We Know Oprah Is a Star," *McCall's*, August 1995, p. 73.

21. "My Most Embarrassing Moment," *Ebony*, September 1987, p. 112.

22. Ibid.

23. Ibid.

24. "My Favorite Quotes," www.ASingh007/Quotes.html.

25. "Oprah Winfrey," *People Weekly*, May 12, 1997, p. 115.

26. Charles L. Sanders, "Oprah Winfrey's Sky-High Home," *Ebony*, October 1988, p. 56.

27. Felicia R. Lee, "Black Art Show's Goal: Recognition and Buyers," *The New York Times*, January 31, 1998.

28. "The 10 Best Places to Live the Good Life," *Mother Earth News*, August 18, 1996, p. 26.

29. "Oprah's Neighbors Apologize for County's Remark," July 4, 1996, www.tvtalkshows.com.

30. Dan Santow, "Christmas at Oprah," *Redbook*, December 1994, p. 82.

31. Ibid.

32. Ibid.

33. Patricia Fisher, "Oprah's Theme: Only Strong Survive," *Newsday*, February 26, 1989, p. 19.

34. Christopher Little, "Oprah Winfrey," *People Weekly*, December 20, 1987, p. 74.

35. Lisa DePaulo, "Oprah's Private Life: The Inside Story," *TV Guide*, June 3, 1989, p. 2.

36. "Oprah Donates $100,000 to Harold Washington Library," *Jet*, October 7, 1991, p. 18.

37. "Donated: By Oprah Winfrey, to Atlanta's Morehouse," *People Online Daily*, November 12, 1997.

38. Press Release, "Woodland Care Center Teams Up with Oprah Winfrey's Angel Network to Build Habitat for Humanity Home in Philadelphia," Woodland Care Center, November 14, 1997.

39. Frank McCleary, "Oprah Gives Chrisman Student a $25,000 Boost," *The Examiner*, May 14, 1998.

40. "Shoes on the Net Joins Forces with *The Oprah Winfrey Show*," www.shoesonthenet.com.

41. Caroline Jeffs, "Oprah Comes to Greencastle," University Wire, DePauw University, September 19, 1997.

42. "Oprah Winfrey: Reveals the Real Reason Why She Stayed on TV," *Jet*, November 24, 1997, p. 59.

43. "Oprah Donates Angels to Museum," January 30, 1997, www.tvtalkshows.com.

44. "Oprah: Don't Drink Her Kool Aid," www.capecod.net/~dfeuilla/Jive-Turkey/Oprah.

On Romance

1. Oprah Winfrey, "TV's Super Women," *Ladies' Home Journal*, March 1988, p. 167.

2. Charles Whitaker, "The Most Talked-About TV Talk Show Host," *Ebony*, March 1987, p. 44.

3. Gretchen Reynolds, "Oprah Unbound," *Chicago*, November 1993, p. 86.

4. Judy Markey, "Brassy, Sassy Oprah Winfrey," *Cosmopolitan*, September 1986, p. 98.

5. "Gayle King Makes Talk Show History with Oprah and Stedman," *Jet*, October 20, 1997, p. 92.

6. Stedman Graham, "Mr. Oprah No More," *McCall's*, March 1997, p. 34.

7. "Oprah Winfrey Celebrates Her 43rd Birthday at Party Hosted by Quincy Jones in LA," *Jet*, April 21, 1997, p. 60.

8. Mark Steyn, "Comic Oprah," *National Review*, March 23, 1998, p. 30.

9. Oprah Winfrey, *Larry King Live*, CNN, January 4, 1995.

10. "For the Love of Mike," *USA Today*, February 23, 1998, p. 2D.

11. R. C. Smith, "She Once Trashed Her Apartment to Make a Point," *TV Guide*, August 30, 1996, p. 31.

12. "Between the Covers," *People*, August 18, 1987, p. 10.

13. "Oprah Winfrey's Success Story," *Ladies' Home Journal*, March 1987, p. 64.

14. "Oprah Winfrey, 32, the Exception that Proves the Rule in Talk Show Hosts," *People Weekly*, August 25, 1986, p. 69.

15. Jackie Rogers, "Understanding Oprah," *Redbook*, September 1993, p. 130.

16. "Oprah Talks About Marriage," 1997, www.tvtalkshows.com.

17. George Mair, *Oprah Winfrey: The Real Story* (Secaucus, N. J.: Birch Lane Press, 1994), p 349.

18. Dana Kennedy, "After a Year of Personal and Professional Turmoil, TV's Richest Woman is Changing Her Life and Her Show," *Entertainment Weekly*, September 9, 1994, p. 20.

19. Jill Brooke Coiner, "Oprah Sets the Record Straight," *McCall's*, November 1993, p. 148.

20. Kinney Littlefield, "Oprah Still Enjoying Her Power," *St. Louis Post-Dispatch*, May 28, 1997, p. 3E.

21. "Oprah Winfrey," *People Weekly*, December 27, 1993.

22. Robert Waldron, *Oprah!* (New York: St. Martin's Press, 1987), p. 198.

23. Elizabeth Sporkin, "Her Man Stedman," *People*, November 23, 1992, p. 136.

24. Joyce Brothers, "What Kind of Wife Will Oprah Winfrey Make?" *Good Housekeeping*, November 1, 1994, p. 68.

25. Maureen Olsen, "Oprah Winfrey," miavx1.muohio.edu/~edupcwis/Olsen_Oprah.html.

26. Jada Pinkett and Will Smith, "The Sexiest Man Alive: Hollywood's Best Boyfriends," *People*, November 17, 1997, p. 155.

27. Karen Thomas, "Out of Oprah's Shadow," *USA Today*, February 28, 1997, p. 1D.

28. Sporkin, "Her Man Stedman," p. 132.

29. Kim Hubbard and Jeanne Gordon, "On Tour: In His Own Write," *People*, April 14, 1997, p. 59.

30. Barbara Geehan, "Retton Pregnant; Baby Due in April," *USA Today*, November 16, 1994, p. 2.

31. Pinkett and Smith, "The Sexiest Man Alive."

32. Thomas, "Out of Oprah's Shadow."

33. Hubbard and Gordon, "On Tour."

34. Ibid.

35. Joshua Levine, "Badass Sells," *Forbes Magazine*, April 21, 1997, p. 142.

36. Hubbard and Gordon, "On Tour."

37. "No Three-Dog Nights," *People*, August 23, 1993, p. 86.

Oprah on the Outside

1. Linda Kramer, "Marathon Woman," *People Weekly*, November 7, 1994, p. 19.

2. Ibid.

3. Amby Burfoot, "Inside Story," *Runner's World*, January 1995, p. 68.

4. Ibid.

5. "Oprah Winfrey Gives Her Weight Loss Tips in New Video, 'Oprah: Make the Connection,' " *Jet*, October 20, 1997, p. 23.

6. John Hanc, "Fitness: Going from Flab to Fit with Oprah," *Newsday*, November 23, 1996, p. E2.

7. Dana Kennedy, "Oprah: Act Two," *Entertainment Weekly*, September 9, 1994, p. 20.

8. "Rack Race," *People Weekly*, July 4, 1994, p. 42.

9. Grace Bennet, "Oprah's Diet: How Her New Plan Can Work for You," *McCall's*, March 1994, p. 38.

10. "Fat Chance," *Entertainment Weekly*, November 25, 1994, p. 12.

11. Gretchen Reynolds, "The Oprah Winfrey Plan," *Runner's World*, March 1995, p. 64.

12. "Telluride, Colorado," *Chicago*, December 1992, p. 111.

13. Gretchen Reynolds, "The Oprah Winfrey Plan."

14. *Oprah Winfrey: Make the Connection*, video, 1997.

15. Esther Zimmerman, "Bring Back the Old Oprah," *Newsday*, December 6, 1988, p. 76.

16. Ellen Byron, "Oprah Invites You to Dinner," *Redbook*, August 1989, p. 102.

17. Gretchen Reynolds, "A Year to Remember: Oprah Grows Up," *TV Guide*, January 7, 1995, p. 14.

18. "Oprah Winfrey and Cher," *Los Angeles Times*, December 11, 1990, p. 8.

19. "Oprah Reveals Her Battle to Stay Slim on Dieting Segment of Her TV Show," *Jet*, December 4, 1989, p. 14.

20. Marcia Ann Gillespie, "Winfrey Takes All," *Ms.*, November 1988, p. 53.

21. Norman King, "Oprah," *Good Housekeeping*, August 1987, p. 179.

22. Richard Zoglin, "People Sense the Realness," *Time*, September 15, 1986, p. 99.

23. Linden Gross, "Oprah Winfrey, Wonder Woman," *Ladies' Home Journal*, December 1988, p. 43.

24. Bob Greene and Oprah Winfrey, "How She Did It," *St. Louis Post-Dispatch*, January 6, 1997, p. 1E.

25. Richard Sanders, "TV Host Oprah Winfrey, Chicago's Biggest Kick, Boots Up for a Star-Making Role in *The Color Purple*," *People Weekly*, December 16, 1995.

26. Bob Greene and Oprah Winfrey, "How She Did It: Winfrey's Fitness Success Is Detailed in a Five-Part Series," *St. Louis Post-Dispatch*, January 6, 1997, p. 1E.

27. Susan King, "Oprah Tackles Weighty Matters in New Video," *The New York Times*, September 29, 1997, p. S14.

28. Paul D. Colford, "Not Just Another Oprah Cover," *Newsday*, March 9, 1995, p. B2.

29. "Chat with Oprah," America Online, October 3, 1995.

30. Bill Brashler, "Next on Oprah . . ." *Ladies' Home Journal*, August 1991, p. 94.

31. Susan L. Taylor, "An Intimate Talk with Oprah," *Essence*, August 1987, p. 57.

32. Jeff Rhoads, "Oprah Dedicates Show to Her Trial Experience," *Globe-News*, February 27, 1998.

33. Oprah Winfrey, Testimony, Senate Judiciary Committee, November 14, 1991.

34. "Big Gain, No Pain," *People*, January 14, 1991, p. 82.

35. Bill Adler, *The Uncommon Wisdom of Oprah Winfrey* (Seacaucus, N.J.: Birch Lane Press, 1997), p. 239.

36. Myrna Blyth, "Advice from Oprah," *Ladies' Home Journal*, February 1995, p. 10.

37. Miriam Kanner, "Oprah at 40: What She's Learned the Hard Way," *Ladies' Home Journal*, February 1994, p. 96.

38. "Big Gain, No Pain."

39. Alex Tresniowski, "Oprah Buff: After Four Years with a New Fitness Philosophy, Oprah Is Happy at Last," *People Weekly*, September 9, 1996, p. 8.

40. Adler, *The Uncommon Wisdom of Oprah Winfrey*, p. 267.

41. Tresniowski, "Oprah Buff," *People*, September 9, 1996. p. 10.

42. Joanna Powell, "I Was Trying to Fill Something Deeper," *Good Housekeeping*, October, 1996, p. 80.

43. "Lady with a Calling," www.Time100.com

44. Jackie Rogers, "Understanding Oprah," *Redbook*, September 1993, p. 132.

45. Stephen Rebello, "Brand Oprah," *Success*, May 1998, p. 64.

46. Patricia Fisher, "Oprah's Theme: Only the Strong Survive," *Newsday*, February 26, 1989, p. 19.

47. "Oprah Winfrey: Entertainment Executive," The Hall of Business Web site, www.achievement.org.

48. Charles Whitaker, "The Most Talked-About TV Talk Show Host," *Ebony*, March 1987, p. 44.

49. Mark Steyn, "Comic Oprah," *National Review*, March 23, 1998, p. 30.

50. "Oprah Winfrey," *People Weekly*, May 12, 1997, p. 115.

51. "Stubby Fingers but Bald No More," Knight Ridder/Tribune News Service, April 9, 1996.

52. Pamela Noel, "Lights! Camera! Oprah!" *Ebony*, April 1985, p. 102.

53. Tornabene, "Here's Oprah," p. 56.

54. Ibid., p. 48.

55. "People," *Newsday*, August 30, 1989, p. 8.

56. Kenneth Best, "Q&A: Gayle King: on Television, for News and Talk, Too," *The New York Times*, March 29, 1998.

57. Melina Gerosa, "Oprah: Fit for Life," *Ladies' Home Journal*, February 1996, p. 180.

58. Mary-Ann Bendel, "TV's Super Women," *Ladies' Home Journal*, March 1988, p. 124.

59. "The Best and Worst Dressed on TV," *TV Guide*, www2.nis.newscorp.com.

Oprah on the Inside

1. Leslie Rubinstein, "Oprah! Thriving on Faith," *McCall's*, August 1987, p. 140.

2. Nichole M. Christian, "Commencements; Speakers Counsel Courage, Perseverance and Hope," *The New York Times*, May 25, 1998.

3. Richard Zoglin, "Lady with a Calling," *Time*, August 8, 1988, p. 64.

4. Rubinstein, "Oprah! Thriving on Faith."

5. Charles Whitaker, "The Most Talked-About TV Talk Show Host," *Ebony*, March 1987, p. 44.

6. Rubinstein, "Oprah! Thriving on Faith."

7. "Upfront Goes to Zip-A-Dee-Doo-Dah Lunch with Oprah," *Chicago*, November 1985, p. 16.

8. Charles L. Sanders, "Oprah Winfrey's Sky-High Home," *Ebony*, October 1988, p. 57.

9. Barbara Grizzuti Harrison, "The Importance of Being Oprah," *The New York Times Magazine*, June 11, 1989, p. 30.

10. Melina Gerosa, "What Makes Oprah Run?" *Ladies' Home Journal*, November 1994, p. 200.

11. Barbara Grizzuti Harrison, "The Importance of Being Oprah," p. 46.

12. Lyn Torrnabene, "Here's Oprah," *Woman's Day*, October 1, 1986, p. 59.

13. Marion Long, "Paradise Tossed," *Omni*, April 1988, p. 106.

14. Chris Anderson, "Meet Oprah Winfrey," *Good Housekeeping*, August 1986, p. 32.

15. Bill Brashler, "Next on Oprah . . ." *Ladies' Home Journal*, August 1991, p. 146.

16. Miriam Kanner, "Oprah at 40: What She's Learned the Hard Way," *Ladies' Home Journal*, February 1994, p. 96.

17. Tananarive Due, "Oprah Shares Her Struggle to Lose Weight in New Video," Knight-Ridder/Tribune News Service, October 2, 1997.

18. Gretchen Reynolds, "Oprah Unbound," *Chicago*, November 1993, p. 86.

19. The Oprah Winfrey Show Web site, Spring 1998.

20. Susan L. Taylor, "An Intimate Talk with Oprah," *Essence*, August 1987, p. 57.

21. Wendy Kaminer, "They Seduce Us by Telling Us What We Want to Hear," *Newsweek*, October 20, 1997.

22. Joanna Powell, "I Was Trying to Fill Something Deeper," *Good Housekeeping*, October 1996, p. 80.

23. Pearl Cleage, "Walking in the Light," *Essence*, June 1991, p. 47.

24. Robert Waldron, *Oprah!* (New York: St. Martin's Press, 1987), p. 102.

25. Stedman Graham, *You Can Make It Happen Every Day* (New York: Simon & Schuster, 1998), p. 133.

26. Maureen Olsen, "Oprah Winfrey," miavx1.muohio.edu/~edpcwis/Olsen_Oprah.html.

27. "Oprah Winfrey—Media Magnate," *Esquire*, December 1989, p. 114.

28. Judy Markey, "Opinionated Oprah," *Woman's Day*, October 4, 1988, p. 60.

29. J. Randy Taraborrelli, "How Oprah Does It All," *Redbook*, August 1996, p. 76.

30. Charles L. Sanders, "Oprah Winfrey's Sky-High Home," *Ebony*, October 1988, p. 57.

31. Gerosa, "What Makes Oprah Run?"

32. Norman King, *Everybody Loves Oprah* (New York: William Morrow and Company, 1987), p. 136.

33. Oprah Winfrey, Commencement Address, Wellesley College, Wellesley, Massachusetts, May 30, 1997.

On Truth and Courage

1. David Rensin, "The Prime Time of Ms. Oprah Winfrey," *TV Guide*, May 16, 1992, p. 11.

2. Diane Sawyer, *ABC 20/20*, March 2, 1998.

3. Pearl Cleage, "Walking in the Light," *Essence*, June 1993, p. 47.

4. Linden Gross, "Oprah Winfrey, Wonder Woman," *Ladies' Home Journal*, December 1988, p. 40.

5. Alex Tresniowski, "Oprah Buff: After Four Years With a New Fitness Philosophy, Oprah Is Happy at Last," *People Weekly*, September 9, 1996, p. 80.

6. Stedman Graham, *You Can Make It Happen Every Day* (New York: Simon & Schuster, 1998), p. 83.

7. "What She Did for Love," *People Weekly*, January 30, 1995, p. 55.

8. "Oprah Reveals on Her Show She Smoked Crack Cocaine During Her 20s," *Jet*, January 30, 1995, p. 51.

9. Myrna Blyth, "Advice from Oprah," *Ladies' Home Journal*, February 1995, p. 10.

10. "What She Did for Love."

11. Patricia Gaines, "Oprah Winfrey Admits Drug Use," *Washington Post*, January 13, 1995, p. C1.

12. Ellen Edwards, "Oprah Winfrey Admits Drug Use," *Washington Post*, January 13, 1995, p. A1.

13. "Oprah Reveals on Her Show."

14. Laura B. Randolph, "Oprah!" *Ebony*, July 1995, p. 22.

15. John Culhane, "Oprah Winfrey: How Truth Changed Her Life," *Reader's Digest*, February 1989, p. 101.

On Doing Right

1. George Mair, *Oprah Winfrey: The Real Story* (Secaucus, N. J.: Birch Lane Press, 1994), p. 344.

2. Belinda Luscombe, "Diving into the Deep End," *Time*, October 7, 1996, p. 101.

3. Julia Cameron, "Simply Oprah," *Cosmopolitan*, February 1989, p. 215.

4. Marion Long, "Paradise Tossed," *Omni*, April 1988, p. 106.

5. Cindy Pearlman, "Civil Servant," *Entertainment Weekly*, March 19, 1993, p. 12.

6. Mark Babineck, Associated Press, February 26, 1998.

7. "Quote of the Day," *The New York Times*, January 21, 1998.

8. Barbara Laker and Theresa Conroy, "Cattle Ranchers Should've Known: Oprah Just Doesn't Lose," *San Diego Union-Tribune*, March 6, 1998, p. E3.

9. "Cattle Producers' Hard Work Pays Off: Oprah Sets Record Straight," Press Release, National Cattlemen's Beef Association, April 24, 1996.

10. Mark Babineck, "Cattleman Says Second Show Not Enough to Halt Beef Price Plunge," Associated Press, *Amarillo Globe-News*, January 26, 1998.

11. Mark Babineck, The Associated Press, February 26, 1998.

12. Diane Sawyer, "A Matter of Principle," *ABC 20/20*, March 2, 1998.

13. "Oprah Says Amarillo Experience 'a Blessing,' " Associated Press, Amarillo, Texas, March 2, 1998.

14. Kathryn Straach, "Oprah Can Play in Amarillo Until the Cows Come Home," *Dallas Morning News*, January 18, 1998, p. 6G.

15. "An Open Letter to Oprah Winfrey from Members of the Cattle Industry," February 19, 1998, www.Vegsource.org.

16. David McLemore, "Oprah on Answering End of Questions at Beef Trial: She Says Talkshow Was for Viewers, Not Cattlemen," *Dallas Morning News*, February 4, 1998, p. 1A.

17. "Oprah in Bad Mood on Mad Cow Show, Witness Testifies," Reuters, January 27, 1998.

18. Marcus Errico, "Oprah's B-day Present: Apology for 'Lynch Mob' Remarks," *E! Online*, January 29, 1998.

19. Aaron Brown, "Oprah Winfrey Verdict," *Good Morning America*, ABC, February 27, 1998.

20. Jeff Franks, "Cattleman to Appeal Verdict in Winfrey Lawsuit," Reuters, February 27, 1998.

21. Paul Katel, "Winfrey Wins Burger War in Texas," *USA Today*, February 27, 1998, p. 3A.

22. "Oprah Winfrey Made Ground Meat of Big Beef in the Heart of Texas Cattle Country Thursday," Associated Press, Amarillo, Texas, February 27, 1998.

23. Stephen Brain, "Jury Rejects Texas Cattleman's Legal Beef with Winfrey," *Los Angeles Times*, February 27, 1996, p. A27.

24. "Feud of the Week," *Time*, January 12, 1998, p. 75.

25. David Bowser, "Oprah Facing Another Trial in Texas Over Bashing Beef," www@lifestockweekly.com.

26. Brown, "Oprah Winfrey Verdict."

27. Mark Babineck, The Associated Press, February 26, 1998.

28. "No Welcome Mat for Oprah," *Los Angeles Times*, January 13, 1998, p. F2.

29. Susan Feeney, "Medal of Freedom Gleams for Pioneering Rights Advocates," *Dallas Morning News*, January 16, 1998, p. 1A.

30. "I'd Marry Oprah Today," *Star*, March 17, 1998, p. 8.

31. John W. Gonzales, "Potential Oprah Jurors Grilled," *Rocky Mountain News*, January 21, 1998, p. 3A.

32. McLemore, "Oprah on Answering End of Questions at Beef Trial."

33. Jeff Rhoads, "Oprah Dedicates Show to Her Trial Experience," *Amarillo Globe-News*, February 27, 1994.

34. "Oprah Says Amarillo Experience 'a Blessing,'" Associated Press, Amarillo, Texas, March 2, 1998.

On Solving the World's Problems

1. Liz Smith, "Oprah Exhales," *Good Housekeeping*, October 1995, p. 120.

2. Shelly Levitt, "Not Scared, Not Silent," *People*, September 7, 1992, p. 49.

3. Mary H. J. Farrell, "Oprah's Crusade," *People*, December 2, 1991, p. 68.

4. "Christmas Presence," *Harper's Bazaar*, December 1990, p. 127.

5. "On Television: Review," *Atlanta Journal*, October 3, 1995.

6. Geoffrey Johnson, Dale Eastman, and Gretchen Reynolds, "Seven Who Made a Difference," *Chicago*, January 1995, p. 48.

7. Ibid.

8. Stephen Rebello, "Brand Oprah," *Success*, May 1998, p. 64.

9. Ibid.

10. Marilyn Johnson and Dana Fineman, "Oprah Winfrey: A Life in Books," *Life*, September 1997, p. 44.

11. Laura B. Randolph, "Oprah!" *Ebony*, July 1995, p. 22.

12. Melina Gerosa, "Oprah: Fit for Life," *Ladies' Home Journal*, February 1996, p. 180.

13. *The Oprah Winfrey Show* Web site, Winter 1998.

14. The Daytime Emmy Awards, NBC Television, May 15, 1998.

15. "Oprah Winfrey: Talk-Show Host," *Time*, June 17, 1996, p. 25.

16. Oprah Winfrey, Speech, 15th Annual Convention, Radio and Television News Directors Association, New Orleans, Louisiana, 1995.

17. Dana Kennedy, "Oprah: Act Two," *Entertainment Weekly*, September 9, 1994, p. 20.

18. Leonard Pitts Jr., "The Queen of Gab Leads a Campaign Against Sleaze TV," Knight-Ridder/Tribune News Service, July 20, 1995.

19. Katharine Kest, "What Oprah Really Wants," *Redbook*, August 1995, p. 77.

20. Trudy S. Moore, "How *The Oprah Winfrey Show* Helps People Live Better Lives," *Jet*, April 18, 1994, p. 56.

21. Randolph, "Oprah!"

22. "Upfront Goes to Zip-A-Dee-Doo-Dah Lunch with Oprah," *Chicago*, November 1985, p. 16.

23. Nellie Bly, *Oprah! Up Close and Down Home* (New York: Zebra Books, 1993), p. 280.

24. Bridget Byrne, "Springer Out-Sleazes Oprah," *E! Online*, March 5, 1998.

Oprah's Worst Mistakes

1. Judy Markey, "Brassy, Sassy Oprah Winfrey," *Cosmopolitan*, September 1986, p. 99.

2. Marjorie Rosen, "Oprah Overcomes," *People Weekly*, January 10, 1994, p. 42.

3. Jill Brooke Coiner, "Oprah Sets the Record Straight," *McCall's*, November 1993, p. 149.

4. Eric Sherman, "Oprah's Wonder Year," *Ladies' Home Journal*, May 1990, p. 157.

5. Harry Levins, "People," *St. Louis Post-Dispatch*, June 19, 1993, p. 4A.

6. "Backing Off from the Book," *People*, July 5, 1993, p. 43.

7. Chris Nashawaty, "Off the Radar: What Happened to These Big Blips on the Hollywood Map," *Entertainment Weekly*, June 9, 1995, p. 8.

8. Laura B. Randolph, "Oprah Opens Up About Her Weight, Her Wedding, and Why She Withheld the Book," *Ebony*, October 1993, p. 131.

9. Nellie Bly, *Oprah! Up Close and Down Home* (New York: Zebra Books, 1993), p. 98.

10. Norman King, *Everybody Loves Oprah* (New York: William Morrow and Company, 1987), p. 194.

11. Luther, Young, "She's Found Success Just by Being Herself," *Baltimore Sun*, January 27, 1985, p. E1.

12. Action Alert, "Tell Oprah to Treat Turkeys Tenderly," www.envirolink.org.

Others Speak About Oprah

1. Curt Schleier, "Donahue Challenged by Oprah Ratings Success," *Advertising Age*, January 19, 1987, p. 30.

2. Stephen Rebello, "Brand Oprah," *Success*, May 1998, p. 65.

3. Paul Noglows, "Oprah: The Year of Living Dangerously," *Working Woman*, May 1994, p. 52.

4. Leonard Pitts, "The Queen of Gab Leads a Campaign Against Sleaze TV," Knight-Ridder/Tribune News Service, July 20, 1995.

5. Rachel's Ode to Oprah Winfrey, www.virtual-space.com.

6. Dana Kennedy, "After a Year of Personal and Professional Turmoil, TV's Richest Woman is Changing Her Life and Her Show," *Entertainment Weekly*, September 9, 1994, p. 20.

7. Nellie Bly, *Oprah! Up Close and Down Home* (New York: Zebra Books, 1993), p. 75.

8. Myrna Blyth, "Advice from Oprah," *Ladies' Home Journal*, February 1995, p. 10.

9. Jeff Jarvis, "Top 10 Oprah," *People Weekly*, September 5, 1998, p. 15.

10. Gretchen Reynolds, "Oprah Unbound," *Chicago*, November 1993, p. 86.

11. Barbara Kleban Mills and Jill Pearlman, "Sexual Perversity in Chicago: Two Actors Gain Indecent Exposure on Oprah, Sally and Geraldo," *People Weekly*, September 19, 1988, p. 62.

12. George Mair, *Oprah: The Real Story* (Secaucus, N. J.: Birch Lane Press, 1994), p. 22.

13. Susan Sachs, "TV Host's Questions Disturb Challenger Families," *Newsday*, November 11, 1987, p. 9.

14. Ibid.

15. "Contrite Oprah Huddles with Jewish Leaders, Condemns Anti-Semitism," *Variety*, May 17, 1989, p. 49.

16. Bill Zehme, "It Came From Chicago," *Spy*, December 1986.

Looking Ahead

1. J. Randy Taraborrelli, "The Change That Has Made Oprah So Happy," *Redbook*, May 1997, p. 94.

2. Robert La Franco, "Piranha Is Good," *Forbes*, October 16, 1995, p. 66.

3. Judy Markey, "Brassy, Sassy Oprah Winfrey," *Cosmopolitan*, September 1986, p. 96.

4. John Culhane, "Oprah Winfrey: How Truth Changed Her Life," *Reader's Digest*, February 1989, p. 10.

5. David Renson, "The Prime Time of Ms. Oprah Winfrey," *TV Guide*, May 16, 1992, p. 11.

6. Ann Saidman, *Oprah Winfrey: Media Success Story* (Minneapolis: Lerner Publications, 1990), p. 38.

7. Barbara Grizzuti Harrison, "The Importance of Being Oprah," *The New York Times Magazine*, June 11, 1989, p. 46.

8. "Oprah: A Heavenly Body?" *U.S. News & World Report*, March 31, 1997, p. 18.

9. Chris Madden, "A Room of Her Own," *Ladies' Home Journal*, November 1997, p. 222.

10. Oprah Winfrey, Speech, American Women's Economic Development Corporation, New York, February 25, 1989.

11. Audrey Edwards, "Stealing the Show," *Essence*, October 1986, p. 123.

12. Oprah Winfrey, Interview with Mike Wallace, *Sixty Minutes*, December 14, 1986.

13. Oprah Winfrey, Commencement Address, Wellesley College, Wellesley, Massachusetts, May 30, 1997.

14. Richard C. Firstman, "Oprah Power," *Newsday*, November 1, 1989, p. 4.

15. Barbara Grizzuti Harrison, "Last Year Oprah Winfrey Made $25 Million," *The New York Times Magazine*, April 14, 1996.

16. Eric Sherman, "Oprah's Wonder Year," *Ladies' Home Journal*, May 1990, p. 220.

17. "Oprah Winfrey," *People Weekly*, December 27, 1993, p. 52.

18. Luchina Fisher, "In Full Stride," *People Weekly*, September 12, 1994, p. 84.

19. Leslie Rubenstein, "Oprah! Thriving on Faith," *McCall's*, August 1987, p. 140.

20. Ben Kubasik, "Five More Years of Talk Show, Says Winfrey," *Newsday*, June 16, 1987, p. 15.

21. Oprah Winfrey, Interview, America Online, October 3, 1995.

22. "Oprah Winfrey Reveals the Real Reason Why She Stayed on TV," *Jet*, November 24, 1997.

23. R. C. Smith, "She Once Trashed Her Apartment to Make a Point," *TV Guide*, August 30, 1986, p. 30.

791.45   Winfrey, Oprah.
Win

Oprah Winfrey
speaks.

DATE			
10-24-0	4/17/14		
11-7-01			
11-28-0			
4/16/10			
2 9 NOV 2012			
12/12/13			

BAKER & TAYLOR